BUILD YOUR OWN

SPORTS CAR

FOR AS LITTLE AS £250 — AND RACE IT!

BUILD YOUR OWN
SPORTS CAR
FOR AS LITTLE AS £250 – AND RACE IT!

RON CHAMPION

SECOND EDITION: Now also covers building a racing version

Haynes Publishing

The plans, drawings and information in this book, and the name Locost, are for private use only and not for commercial enterprise.

All rights reserved. No part of this publication may be reproduced, stored in a retrieval system or transmitted, in any form or by any means, electronic, mechanical, photocopying, recording or otherwise, without prior permission in writing from Haynes Publishing.

First edition published by G.T. Foulis in 1996
Reprinted regularly in 1996, 1997, 1998 and 1999
Second edition, expanded and reformatted in full colour, published by Haynes Publishing in May 2000

A catalogue record for this book is available from the British Library.

ISBN 1 85960 636 9

Library of Congress catalog card no. 99-85875

Photographs courtesy the author except where credited.

Published by Haynes Publishing, Sparkford, Nr Yeovil, Somerset BA22 7JJ
Tel: 01963 440635 Fax: 01963 440001
Int. tel: +44 1963 440635 Fax: +44 1963 440001
E-mail: sales@haynes-manuals.co.uk
Web site: www.haynes.co.uk

Haynes North America Inc.,
861 Lawrence Drive, Newbury Park,
California 91320, USA.

Designed & typeset by G&M, Raunds, Northamptonshire
Printed and bound in Great Britain by J.H. Haynes & Co. Ltd, Sparkford

WARNING

While every attempt has been made throughout this book to emphasise the safety aspects of building your own car, the publishers, the author and the distributors accept no liability whatsoever for any damage, injury or loss resulting from the use of this book. If you have any doubts about your ability to <u>safely</u> build your own car then it is recommended that you seek advice from a professional engineer.

Jurisdictions which have strict emission control laws may consider any modification to a vehicle to be an infringement of those laws. You are advised to check with the appropriate body or authority whether your proposed modification complies fully with the law. The publishers accept no liability in this regard.

Contents

Acknowledgements

Very few tasks are completed without the help of others. This book is no exception, and I would like to record my thanks to the many people who have kindly availed me of their advice and assistance in bringing it about.

My special thanks go to my wife Mary. She has helped me enormously, and I am grateful to her for her patience in putting up with the inevitable piles of papers that have littered the family home for so long.

My thanks, too, go to Ron Fitzwater for valued technical guidance, to Steve Williams and Janet Pullan who took many of the photographs which appear in the book, to R.G. Smith for his help with the wiring diagram, to my son James, for his valuable assistance in constructing the prototype Locost, to the 750 Motor Club for their help, particularly Robin Knight, Neil Carr-Jones and Mike Topp (three times 750 Motor Club kit car champion, whose enthusiasm for the Locost has meant we now have a race series), to Rory Perrett, Chairman of the Locost Club, who has made it the fastest growing kit car club in the UK and extended it to America, Australia, New Zealand, Norway and Sweden, to Ian Gray and Martin Keenan for their development work which has made the Locost project more achievable for new builders by supplying chassis and other parts, to Ken Walton who has promoted the Locost movement in the USA, and to my mum who is my biggest fan.

Last but not least, my thanks to John Hardaker, my editor, whose hard work and skill helped to make this book possible.

Preface to new edition

When I was writing the original edition of this book I was quietly confident that the prospect of being able to build your own sports car for as little as £250 would capture the imagination of quite a few people, but I couldn't have guessed back in 1996 that it would turn out to be the sustained bestseller that it has proved to be for my publisher, and I certainly could not have predicted what its publication has led to. It has scratched the surface to reveal a rich vein of engineering talent, and I am amazed at the ingenuity that builders have shown in interpreting my basic plans – no two cars are the same.

The ever growing numbers of Locost builders, both in the UK and overseas, led to the formation of the Locost Car Club, with a regular Newsletter, regional rallies and an increasing camaraderie between Locosters, many of whom are in touch with each other through the Internet. A progression from this has been the appearance of small companies supplying made-up chassis, suspension units and other parts for would-be builders too keen to get going than 'waste' time learning to weld.

Then the RAC racing committee spotted the car's potential as a club-level racer, and 1999 saw the start of the Locost Series run by the 750 Motor Club with meetings at

A 'plague' of Locosts at the author's home. (Photo. Steve Williams)

five different circuits in the UK and the very real prospect of a Championship from 2000 onwards. This presents an opportunity to enjoy all the excitement of motor racing at relatively low cost, and to learn the skills of chassis design, performance improvement and, not least, racecraft. This edition includes a new chapter all about racing a Locost.

The coming of the Single Vehicle Approval scheme and its stringent regulations (mandatory from 1 July 1998) has had its impact on Locost builders who now have to pay close attention to the requirements as laid out in the *SVA Inspection Manual* to ensure that they pass muster at the new test centres and get their obligatory Minister's Approval Certificate to enable their cars to be registered. Many have already successfully got their cars through the test, and this new edition of *Build Your Own Sports Car* has been revised throughout to try to ensure that it is SVA compliant.

The book's success seems also to have had a marked effect on the scrapyard stock of Mark II Ford Escorts. Back in 1996 it was commonplace to see them stacked high, but they are not now nearly so plentiful and scrap dealers have realised they have a ready market amongst Locost builders. Prices have reflected this and you may be asked somewhere between £75 and £125 for your Escort donor car, but bargains are still to be had.

Of course, it doesn't have to be a Ford Escort. I have seen cars built using the full engine and running gear from rear-wheel-drive Fiats, Vauxhalls, MGBs, etc., and a lot of builders have mixed components from a variety of donor vehicles, such as Rover V8 engines with Ford running gear and gearboxes. In one case a Mazda rotary engine and gearbox with MGB running

At the 2000 Autosport International Racing Car Show, Haynes announced its sponsorship of the Locost Race Series, run by the 750 Motor Club. Photographed (from left), Haynes Group Chief Executive Max Pearce presents a £5,000 cheque to the club's racing competition secretary Robin Knight, Locost Formula official Mike Topp, and club chairman Mike Whatley. Patrick Pearce is in the car. (Photo. Steve Williams)

Honda FireBlade-powered Locost under construction by James Champion. (Photo. Martin Thone)

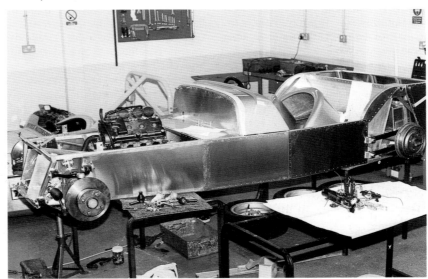

gear was used, and I have even seen a front-wheel-drive transverse engine dropped into the rear compartment. To me the most exciting so far are a couple of motorcycle-engined Locosts, complete with sequential gearboxes, the power to weight ratio of which results in 0–60 in four seconds! So, the world is your oyster.

Ron Champion, 2000

Introduction

I developed an interest in motor cars as a teenager in the '50s when, if you wanted a cheap sports car, the normal thing to do was to buy an Austin Seven or Ford Popular, throw the saloon body away and build your own two-seater sports body.

It was possible to find plenty of scrap electrical conduit on demolition or bomb sites with which to make the framework. This was welded up with an ex-War Department arc welder and, with the aid of tin snips and pop rivets, it was clad in aluminium sheet. As our skills were limited we could only make the body with single curves, but I remember one of the best looking cars of my contemporaries was made with sections of an old wartime fighter aluminium drop tank, which gave him a superb body shape with lots of compound curves.

If one had the money, there was the option to buy a glassfibre body to fit the rolling chassis from Rochdale Engineering for £47 10s., but in my circle of friends this represented four months' wages! We were fortunate in those days that most towns had a Government war surplus shop which sold everything from tank aerials (for making into fishing rods) and aircraft instruments (easily adapted for our specials) to sheepskin flying jackets (ideal for unheated open cars). All of these were more affordable on my weekly wage of £3 10s.

A few of my friends joined the 750 Motor Club and entered their Austin-based specials in the regular club motor races. The rest of us offered practical and moral support as race mechanics, timekeepers, pushers and tea makers. Our involvement gave us all the opportunity to exchange ideas and barter, not only for spares but also for our skills. Our specials became more professional looking, fast and fairly reliable, all on minimal funds. It was very much a case of: if you want it, then make it!

Some of the owner/builders, such as Colin Chapman, progressed to national acclaim. He developed his Austin special into the Lotus Six, then the Lotus Seven – and the rest is history. The Lotus Seven is still being built today, virtually unchanged visually, by Caterham Cars Ltd.

Since the early '80s there has been a tremendous revival in special building, or I should say kit car building. They are mostly based on donor parts, just like those in the '50s, but the main difference is that all the parts are sourced, fabricated, painted, chromed and delivered as a package together with a builder's manual.

My son had been visiting kit car shows, buying kit car magazines and was becoming interested in building his own sports car. Having obtained brochures with prices from several companies, he realised that he would not be able to afford any of the kits in the near or distant future – certainly not until he had completed his education. In our discussions about this I suggested, 'Why buy the kit? I bet we could make one for about £250.' And make one we did. Ever conscious of our low budget, we named our project car 'Lowcost', and later shortened it to 'Locost'.

This book tells you how to make the Locost. It is compiled from the data I collected during the construction of my son's car and the later building of several more Locosts in my capacity as a teacher of motor engineering at a public boarding school. Since its first publication, builders of Locosts have proliferated worldwide and I have yet to find two cars which have been made exactly alike. You have total freedom to adopt and adapt the basic plans to suit your circumstances and purposes.

One thing that the school-built cars have in common is that they were all built by unskilled young people who had hardly ever wielded a spanner and certainly could not weld before joining the Locost project. This has already inspired many – young and not so young – to build their own sports

An Austin Seven special, typical of those built in the 1950s and early 1960s.

cars. If they can do it, so can you!

What the book does not cover is the overhaul and rebuild of the major components – like the engine, gearbox, axle and brakes – because our Locost budget does not include this, and all of the information needed is already available in the Haynes series of workshop manuals. So, unless you are planning on spending a lot more, it is essential to ensure that your donor vehicle is mechanically sound. We have to allow for the cost of normal servicing, though. It would be false economy to build your car without changing the oil, filters, plugs, brake pads and linings, etc.

The advantage of building your car from scratch is that, unlike buying a proprietary kit, you do not have a huge expenditure initially. You can spread the cost of parts and materials over as long a period as you like. You can work on the project in clearly defined modules. You could build the fuel tank first, possibly as a project at evening classes if you are learning to weld. You might choose to start by visiting autojumbles and collecting parts such as instruments or lights. Although likely to cost more, you could buy the parts like the engine, radiator and axle separately, which would save the bother of dismantling a scrap Ford Escort at home, then having to dispose of a rusty shell.

There is no best way to tackle this project but, whatever you do, work safely. If you haven't got one, make your first purchase a first-aid kit, and keep it in your work area. Clear goggles are essential, as are stout footwear, gloves and a protective overall. Never, never work in a T-shirt and trainers.

WHAT DO YOU GET?

In terms of time, effort and money, you will get out of your Locost project as much as you are prepared to put into it, which is like a lot of things in life. It's a fact that, even with very little money, if you have a lot of time to invest you can still put your Locost on the road in a safe and efficient manner.

Here are some examples of cost saving:

- If you cannot afford it why paint it? They look good in polished aluminium (but in the log book describe the colour as silver).

- Do you need a windscreen and surround? If not, you can save the extra cost of windscreen supports, wiper motor, wipers and washers; but you will need a pair of goggles, or a wind deflector mounted on the dashboard top.

- In the '50s and '60s most specials only had a fuel tank dipstick and did without a fuel gauge, sender unit, etc.

- Why bother with wide magnesium wheels when the donor Ford Escort wheels will be fine.

Are you getting the idea? The Locost can be built exactly how you want it and according to how much you can afford.

My son's car *did* eventually have chromed suspension, but he did a paper round to pay for it. We *did* find some wide magnesium wheels – a set for £15 in a local scrapyard, and we *did* find a windscreen at the Beaulieu autojumble for £12.50. His car is still without a hood, but he has never minded the rain too much. He will probably be adding to and upgrading the specification of his car for many years to come. It is a hobby which possibly will also start for you now that you have acquired this book.

THE MOST COMMONLY ASKED QUESTIONS

Q **How fast does it go?**
A My son's car has a 948cc BMC 'A' series engine – as fitted to an Austin A35, Morris Minor and 'Frogeye' Austin Healy Sprite – which will do about 85mph. Obviously the mph rises according to the engine used. For example:

1100cc Ford – 100mph
1300cc Ford – 105mph
1600cc Ford – 120mph
2000cc twin-cam Fiat – 130mph

Q **Is it like a kit car?**
A Most definitely not. Although all the major mechanical components come from one donor vehicle, almost everything else is hand-built from scratch.

Q **How long does it take to make?**
A It's very difficult to say. To actually build it took us about 450 hours, but it is possible that it took that long again to strip and clean the parts from the donor car and to find all the other parts.

Q **Is it expensive to insure?**
A No, because there are specialist companies who are accustomed to dealing with this sort of vehicle, working on the basis that an owner/builder who has taken this much time and effort to build a car is going to use it carefully. They would also assume that owners would undertake any accident repair themselves.

Q **Is it safe?**
A Yes. The chassis is incredibly strong and, just as important, the handling, steering and braking are so good that most potential accident situations can be that much better avoided.

Q **How many miles per gallon?**
A It depends on which engine you fit. The 948cc engine will give you about 50mpg, and the 1600cc Ford engine still gives you over 40mpg. The main reasons for its good fuel consumption are its light weight and low wind resistance (drag factor).

DO'S AND DON'TS

DO read this book from start to finish before starting the project.

DO check the up-to-date regulations for road cars, and if you aim to go racing make sure you obtain the up-to-date race regulations from the 750 Motor Club.

DO ensure that your welding is up to standard before starting work.

DO purchase a first-aid kit and keep it in your work area.

DO wear proper protective overalls, footwear, gloves and correct goggles.

DO seek professional advice if in doubt about safety related matters like brake components and steering.

DO ensure that any vehicle you work on is well supported on axle stands.

DO ensure that all extension leads and cables on any powered equipment are sound and free of cuts and damage, and check that the correct fuse is fitted.

DO keep your work area neat and tidy, with no tripping hazards.

DON'T weld without a fire extinguisher close by.

DON'T work under vehicles supported by jacks, bricks, breeze blocks, etc.

DON'T allow any inflammable substances to be stored in the workshop where you are welding or grinding, and this includes oily rags.

PART 1

SKILLS AND TOOLS

CHAPTER 1

Skills required

I have found that enthusiasm breeds skills, and during my many years as an engineering instructor I have seen time and again that if someone really wants to do something, they find that, with application, they *can* do it. Since you have bought this book, though, I assume it is more likely than not that you already have some basic mechanical skill and knowledge. If this isn't the case, all is not lost, as there are several ways (formally and informally) to acquire the skills you will need.

First and foremost, in building your sports car on a minimal budget, the most important skill you are going to need is patience, as it will take time to source the materials and parts, and build everything yourself. Patience is also an essential aspect of learning to weld.

WELDING

This is a skill you can teach yourself from instruction books and by practising on metal scrap, though most will benefit from professional tuition. Equipment suppliers are generally prepared to give basic instruction to new purchasers of welding equipment.

There are also several training centres specialising in welding, and most technical colleges and further education institutes offer evening classes in all types of welding and metal fabrication. Some actually run courses specifically designed to teach all the skills needed in motor vehicle restoration work.

Booklets containing useful information on equipment and safety procedures can be obtained from the BOC Group, and that company also produces a range of training videos. (Contact BOC Gases, The Priestley Centre, 10 Priestley Road, Surrey Research Park, Guildford, Surrey GU2 5XY. Phone: 01483 579857.)

When buying second-hand, be sure that the vendor gives you a satisfactory demonstration of the equipment in use. He may also be prepared to give you some basic instruction as well.

Even if you already have experience of welding, it is essential to familiarise yourself with the equipment and materials you will be using. I have been welding for over 30 years, but when using an unfamiliar welding set I always try a test weld on a piece of scrap, preferably an offcut from the material I am about to use. It would be a good idea to make up a rectangle or a cube from the RHS (rectangular hollow section) tube you will be using to make the space-frame for your car, and keep practising until your joints are perfect.

There are three basic types of welding – gas, MIG and arc.

SAFETY PRECAUTIONS WHEN WELDING

- **Keep the area clear of combustible material.**

- **Always wear the correct eye protection.**

- **Wear strong boots and gloves, and thick overalls to protect yourself against sparks.**

- **Keep a suitable fire extinguisher close by.**

- **Do not allow electric welding sets to become wet or damp.**

- **Weld in a well-ventilated area and avoid breathing in fumes.**

- **Keep children and pets away from the work area.**

- **Keep oil and grease away from oxy-acetylene equipment.**

- **Keep cylinders upright and secured.**

- **Always turn off the gas supply and mains electricity when not in use.**

Gas welding

This is traditional oxy-acetylene welding, a method developed by the French at the beginning of the century using the two gases oxygen and acetylene. The advantage is that this method does not need a supply of electricity, so it can be used anywhere. The main supplier of oxy-acetylene equipment in the UK is the BOC Group, and while you can purchase torches, hoses and gauges, the gas cylinders can only be rented. Ideal for small jobs is the BOC Portapak.

It is vitally important to follow the correct safety procedures when using pressurised cylinders, and for new users this needs to become a habit from the beginning. Gas cylinders are colour-coded – acetylene cylinders are maroon and oxygen cylinders are black. Acetylene smells of garlic and burns with a smoky yellow-orange flame, but when correctly mixed with oxygen an incredibly hot flame is produced.

Make sure the equipment you are using is fitted with flashback arresters to prevent flames travelling back into the cylinders. Pressure regulators are screwed into the cylinder valves – in the case of acetylene cylinders a left-hand thread is used, and for oxygen cylinders it is a right-hand thread. The hoses connecting the pressure regulators to the torch are red for acetylene and blue for oxygen. Check that the hoses are of best quality and in good condition (do not use them if there are signs of wear), and have hose check valves fitted.

Always keep gas welding equipment free from oil and grease, follow the supplier's instructions when assembling and, when assembled, check for leaks. I use a cup of soapy water and a paint brush to brush the water over the joints. If there are any leaks, they will show as bubbles. If you do detect a leak it can quite often be cured by a further 'nip' with a spanner, but if this doesn't work and you are quite sure all the threads were clean, do not tamper

Fig. 1.1. Gas welding equipment. The taller cylinder (black) contains oxygen and the shorter stouter one to its right (maroon) contains acetylene, both securely supported on a welding trolley. Pay particular attention to the operator's protective overall and gas welding goggles, which are essential, as is the putting on of a pair of thick gloves before starting work. (Photo. Steve Williams)

with it – take the cylinder back to the supplier and have it checked. Do not overtighten any of the joints as most of the fittings are made of brass and the threads are easy to strip.

Before you get started be sure that your work area is free from any combustible material, such as oily rags, fuel tanks, etc., and that it is well ventilated. See also that your cylinders are secured in an upright position (preferably chained on a trolley), and wear the correct welding goggles and gloves.

Having familiarised yourself with the operating instructions and set the gas pressures for the steel thickness you are going to work on (all shown in the BOC booklet), open the acetylene valve and light your torch with the spark igniter.

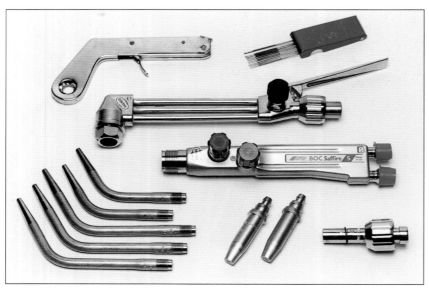

Fig. 1.2. A spark gun, set of nozzle cleaners, a torch, mixer and welding and cutting nozzles. (Photo. Steve Williams)

Adjust the acetylene flame until the smoke just disappears, then open the oxygen valve until you achieve a clearly defined very light blue central flame. This central flame will be surrounded by a darker blue outer flame which shows you are using equal amounts of both gases. This is known as a neutral flame – ideal for welding steel.

If you are right-handed, hold the welding rod in your left hand and start on the right-hand side of the joint to be welded. If you are left-handed, hold the welding rod in your right hand and start on the left side of the joint. Bring the flame to a little over ⅛in from the joint, and hold the nozzle at about 70 degrees. Through your goggles you will see the steel turn into a molten pool. The welding rod tip is introduced into the molten steel where it will also melt and mix. You then move the flame along the joint, allowing the molten pool and welding rod to mix as you go.

Although it will take some time to fully master the art of oxy-acetylene welding your space-frame chassis, once you have done so it is a satisfying though slow process.

MIG welding
MIG (metal inert gas) welding is, in my opinion, the best method for welding your chassis and other parts needing to be fabricated. I have instructed many people in this skill, and my student success rate has been 100 per cent. My usual method is to give direct one-to-one instruction for 30 minutes, familiarising the student with the controls and the techniques. I then given them a quiet work area with the MIG equipment, a big box of steel offcuts of all shapes and thicknesses, and leave them to practise. I check their progress from time to time during the day, advising and demonstrating as necessary, and by the end of the day everyone, without exception so far, has been sufficiently competent to weld a space-frame chassis. By the time the chassis is finished, they should be skilled and confident enough to fabricate suspension components, modify axles and all the other fabrication required. I firmly believe that, with the set of instructions provided with a new MIG welder, a person can teach himself/herself to MIG weld, and the availability of small, low-priced MIG welding equipment has brought welding well within the scope of the DIY enthusiast.

Small MIG welders are available from some car accessory shops and tool shops, and the throwaway gas cylinders involved can be purchased over the counter for just a few pounds. Hiring is an alternative, and if you have your chassis tubes already cut to length it should be possible to fabricate the space-frame over a weekend, thereby keeping hire costs to a minimum.

All welding is basically the same, but with a MIG welder you need an electric power supply. The equipment's controls should be set according to the instructions, but basically you have the power (or amperage) set low for thin steel and high for thick steel. The welding wire is on a spool or drum and is fed through a tube to a nozzle which is held close to the joint to be welded. When you squeeze the trigger on the handgrip it activates a motor which feeds the wire through the nozzle to the joint. The material to be welded is attached to the welding equipment by an earth lead, so as soon as the wire touches the material it completes the circuit causing an electric arc. The wire and two pieces of metal to be joined immediately melt into a small pool and fuse together. Whilst this is happening, gas (either carbon dioxide or a carbon dioxide/argon mix – both being inert gases) from the cylinder attached to the machine also flows from the nozzle under pressure to surround the weld area, excluding any impurities from the immediate atmosphere and cooling the weld area. If you let go of the trigger, the arc, wire and gas flow stop, ready to be restarted by squeezing the trigger again. The arcing creates a very bright light, so your eyes must be protected by a special face mask. This mask will also protect your face from the ultraviolet light given off. The effects are rather like sunburn, so protect your hands with thick gloves, and also protect any other exposed skin. Keep children and animals well away, and if you have helpers or observers, provide them with face masks, too.

The only time I have experienced problems with MIG welding is

Fig. 1.3. A portable MIG welder. A full-face shield (like the one shown in Fig. 1.4) must be used to protect you from the ultraviolet light given off. Thick gloves should also be used to stop your hands getting burnt. (Photo. Steve Williams)

impossible – but remember what I said about the need for patience.

Arc welding is not unlike MIG welding as both use an electric arc to melt the metal to be joined, but instead of a continuous spool of wire, the arc welder uses rods, and instead of gas the rods are coated in a special flux which melts with the rod. When the weld has cooled the flux remains on the surface and needs to be chipped away with a special pointed hammer (a chipping hammer) to expose what, it is hoped, is a good weld beneath.

ENGINEERING SKILLS

If you have selected your donor vehicle well, you should have no need to get into rebuilding the engine, gearbox or axle, but you will have to overhaul and bleed brakes, install a wiring loom, and fit fuel pipes, etc. All the information you need will be in the Haynes manual for your donor vehicle, but you may like to back up this knowledge with evening classes at your local technical college or by joining a local motor club where you will meet like-minded people who might well be interested in your project, and who may be able to help with knowledge, skills, practical help and even the loan of tools and equipment. Also, there is now a thriving Locost Car Club with a regular Newsletter. The Club was started by amateur car builders who read the first edition of this book and went on to make their own sports cars, and it continues to grow in membership, with technical support and advice forthcoming.

PANEL BEATING

This is ideally suited to DIY and should not present any problems. The Locost has been designed with either flat sheet metal skinning or at the worst simple single curvatures which can be formed by hand. Needless to say, you must be able to measure and mark out accurately, but no more so than when cutting wallpaper, and the aluminium sheet can be cut with tin snips, which are like big scissors.

when working outside in windy conditions when poor welds can result because the gas shield is blown away. You can overcome this to some extent by turning up the gas pressure or, if that fails, by making a windbreak – sometimes just standing a box, or the welder itself, on the windy side is enough.

Arc welding

Although small arc welders are very cheap to buy or hire, it takes a long time to develop the necessary skills (though not as long as with gas welding) and it is not really suitable for thin steel. The 16swg tubes for your chassis are about as thin as you can go with an arc welder, and whilst an experienced welder would make a good strong job of it, an inexperienced welder could well have difficulty with such thin material, and I would not recommend welding your chassis as a first job. However, it is not

Fig. 1.4. An arc welder. This equipment uses flux-coated rods and, as with MIG welding, it is essential that thick gloves and a full-face shield (such as the one shown) are used. (Photo. Steve Williams)

PAINTING

When the chassis is complete it can be brush painted. Although I can spray paint, I still brush paint the chassis, mainly because spraying a space-frame is so wasteful of paint – there are more 'holes' than tubes. Since the bodywork is aluminium the question arises whether it is really necessary to paint it, as polished aluminium can look very attractive. If you do decide to paint it, remember that aluminium needs to be etch primed first. You can then hire a compressor and spray gun to apply the top coat, or use aerosol spray cans (one young builder did it this way using 32 cans and it looked very effective).

UPHOLSTERY

Since upholstery in the Locost is very basic it doesn't call for any special skills, and one of the best solutions is to modify salvaged seating from other cars. The interior panels are just hardboard with vinyl stuck on, and floor covering can be made from rubber mats cut to shape.

GLASSFIBRE MOULDING

This is a skill within the scope of the average DIY enthusiast; the main requirement being patience and a clean, well-ventilated work area. A number of readers will have had experience of glassfibre moulding from school (maybe making canoes), but, if not, it is something you can 'have a go at'. Advice and technical assistance is available from glassfibre material suppliers, and I know of at least two suppliers who will give one-day practical training sessions for a modest fee. Also, technical colleges and adult education centres may offer evening classes in glassfibre moulding.

Many Locost builders to date have not had to make their own glassfibre panels, instead using ready-made steel or glassfibre cycle-type trailer wings which come in a number of widths and diameters to fit various wheel sizes. Incidentally, they make ideal moulds if you still wish to make your own wings.

There are at least a dozen kit or production cars of similar design which use a nose cone almost identical to that used on the Locost, and quite often these can be found advertised either new or second-hand in the specialist magazines or at autojumbles. Also, with the growing number of Locost builders, there are now suppliers who manufacture mudguards and nose cones specifically designed for the Locost. Naturally, sourcing requirements in these ways will add to the production cost of your car.

CHAPTER 2

Tools and equipment

This chapter lists all the tools and equipment required to build your Locost. I am acutely aware that we are producing a budget sports car, and that the cost of tools and equipment could exceed the cost of the finished project, but you will probably have a few of these tools already, or possibly you can borrow or hire them.

Included are several tools which, although not essential, will certainly enable you to tackle certain things more quickly and easily.

If you have to purchase tools, my advice is to buy the best you can afford, whether new or second-hand. If you look after them they will last a lifetime. Indeed, a large proportion of my hand tools belonged to my father and father-in-law. Remember, the best are not necessarily new. In fact, most of my metalworking tools and measuring equipment have been purchased second-hand for just a few pounds, and I would not have got more effective or accurate tools had I bought them new.

BUY OR HIRE?
Most towns these days have hire shops, and I think it is worth considering hiring power tools or welding equipment, but for small hand-tools it is best to purchase your own, particularly if you can find good second-hand examples.

Car boot sales and autojumbles are the best source of second-hand tools and equipment. At these places it is expected of you to haggle, which is all part of the fun. Advertisements in local papers are also quite good for second-hand bargains. I have found not only tools, but tyres, radiators, instruments and complete donor cars through such ads. One person I know who built a Locost, bought a second-hand MIG welder, built his car, then sold the welder for a profit – that's enterprise for you!

The most important advice I can give you is to take your time collecting tools, equipment, materials and parts. There have been times when I have spent weeks looking for that elusive item, then after having purchased it new, a similar one has turned up at a fraction of the price I paid. So, remember, more haste – less cash saved!

BASIC HAND-TOOLS
A very basic toolkit would comprise:

Socket set
Set of ring spanners

Fig. 2.1. Socket sets and a set of ring spanners. A selection of different lengths of socket-set extensions is useful. Keeping your sockets on bars, as shown, will make it easier to select them for use and prevent them becoming lost. (Photo. Steve Williams)

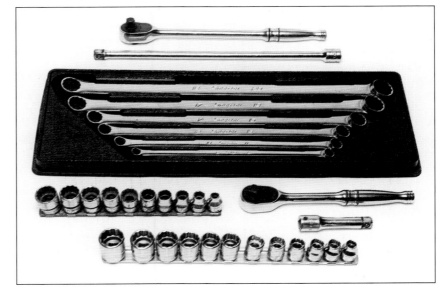

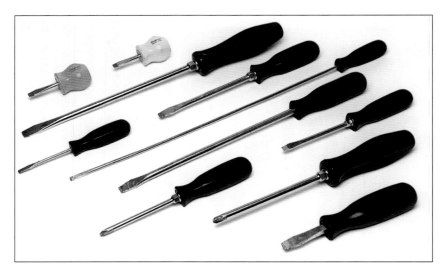

Fig. 2.2. A useful selection of screwdrivers. (Photo. Steve Williams)

Set of open-ended spanners
A small selection of screwdrivers
A selection of pliers
A selection of clamps
A selection of hammers
Steel ruler and set square
Tin snips
Hacksaw
Files – one flat, one round
Pop rivet gun
Wire brush
Cold chisels and punch

Although not essential, a metal guillotine is a useful tool to have.

ESSENTIAL POWER TOOLS
Electric drill
Welding set

BENCH TOOLS
Vice (a Record No. 5 or 6, for example)
Bench drill

Your Locost can be built with just the above tools plus a few basic household items such as scissors, for cutting out card patterns, etc., and pencil or chalk for marking out.

With regard to hand files, I would be the first to admit that an angle grinder could speed the job up considerably, as it can remove as much unwanted metal in a minute as a hand file can in an hour, but when keeping to a tight budget we have to remember that elbow grease is free.

MEASURING AND MARKING
A ruler and set square are the two basic tools of metal working. Anything you produce without these will not be accurate. The ruler I use most of all is made of steel, one yard long and one inch wide. I purchased it many years ago for a few pence from a market stall selling second-hand tools. With some fine wire wool, rust was quickly removed and it has been used almost daily ever since. A small 6in steel ruler, ½in wide, is useful for work in restricted places.

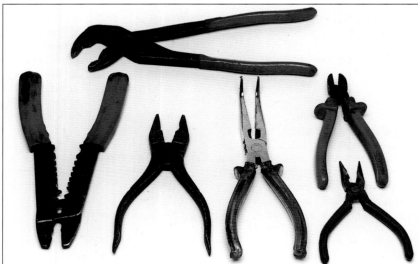

Fig. 2.3. A selection of pliers, including wire strippers and wire cutters. (Photo. Steve Williams)

Fig. 2.4. Wire brushes. (Photo. Steve Williams)

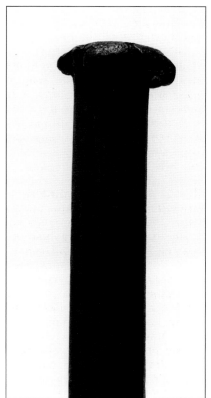

Fig. 2.5. Chisels and punches. Ensure that chisels and punches are kept sharp for accurate marking and punching. (Photo. Steve Williams)

Fig. 2.6. Never use a chisel with a 'mushroomed' head like this as serious injury can be caused by flying fragments. (Photo. Steve Williams)

Fig. 2.7. A correctly dressed, and safe, chisel head. (Photo. Steve Williams)

A 10ft (3m) retractable steel tape measure is very handy to have – it helps you measure around curves and it fits neatly in your pocket for those trips to scrapyards, etc.

Set squares come in a variety of types and sizes, the only one I had for many years was a 12in x 6in (305mm x 152mm) carpenter's square, and this was used to build several Locost space-frame chassis most accurately. I subsequently acquired a 24in x 18in (600mm x 450mm) roofing square which is

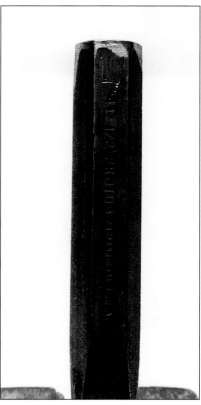

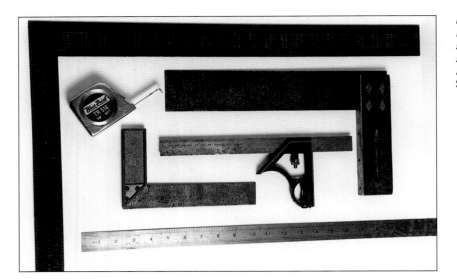

Fig. 2.8. Measuring equipment. A roofer's set square, a retractable steel tape measure, a carpenter's set square, a combination square and a 24in steel ruler. (Photo. Steve Williams)

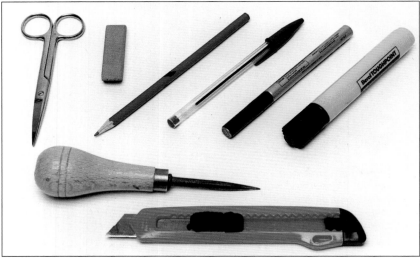

Fig. 2.9. Cutting and marking tools for cardboard templates, etc. (Photo. Steve Williams)

proving invaluable for marking out larger areas. A combination square is a useful tool as it comes with a protractor head for measuring angles, and it also has a spirit level incorporated. If I have been away from my home workshop I have often improvised and checked squareness with the edge of a notebook or have made a quick triangle with an offcut of steel or aluminium sheet.

A centre punch is needed to mark metal for drilling holes. It makes a small indentation when struck with a hammer: essential to centralise the drill bit. But think carefully before using it to mark outer panels such as a bonnet, because it could blemish an otherwise perfect finish.

You will need a scriber for marking out metal, and one can be made from a broken or old screwdriver by grinding or filing the end to a point.

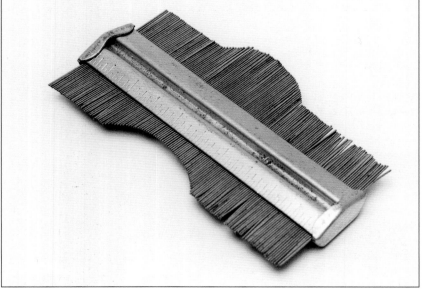

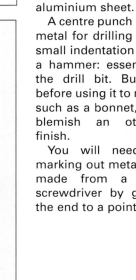

Fig. 2.10. A profile gauge. (Photo. Steve Williams)

CUTTING AND SHAPING

Metal snips are really heavy duty scissors – the two meeting blades shearing the metal. If buying second-hand, take a few postcard sized offcuts of sheet steel with you to try them out on. People often abuse metal snips by cutting steel thicker than they were designed for. This damages the blades and the pivot pin. Standard metal snips will cut up to 16swg; thicker than that will require a guillotine. Although I have several pairs of standard snips, I have hardly used them since acquiring my aviation snips. As the name implies, these were developed for the aviation industry. There are three types: red-handled left cut snips for use anti-clockwise with the waste metal curling to the right, green-handled right cut snips for clockwise use with the waste cut away to the left, and yellow-handled for cutting in a straight line. Unlike the scissor-

Fig. 2.11. Aviation snips for cutting sheet metal. The green-handled snips are used for cutting to the right, the red ones for cutting to the left and the yellow ones for cutting straight. (Photo. Steve Williams)

Fig. 2.12. A sheet metal cutting chisel. A special tool which comes in handy (along with a hammer) for cutting out sections from in situ panels – at a breaker's yard, for instance. (Photo. Steve Williams)

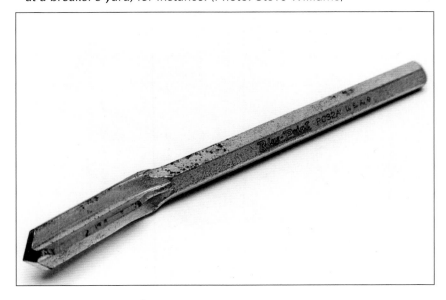

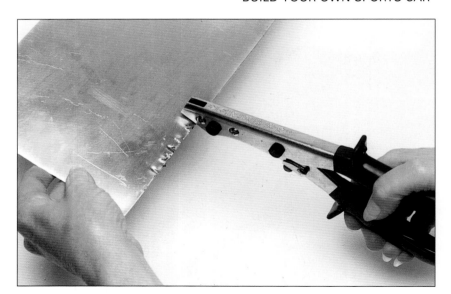

Fig. 2.13. A hand-operated panel nibbler which can be used instead of tin snips in many cases. (Photo. Steve Williams)

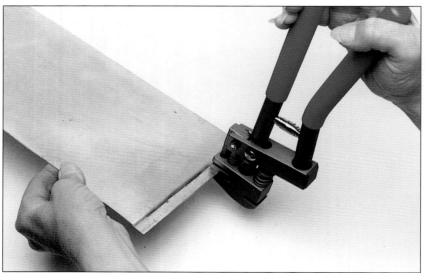

Fig. 2.14. Known as a 'joddler' this tool will create a flange at the edge of sheet metal for an overlapping panel. (Photo. Steve Williams)

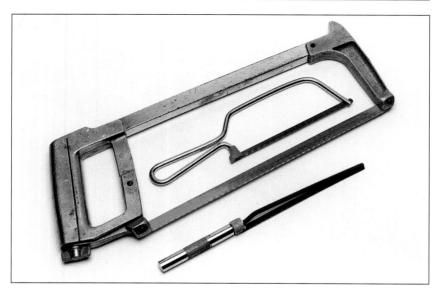

Fig. 2.15. Metal-cutting saws. Large hacksaw, 'Junior' hacksaw, and a very useful handle for holding a 'Junior' hacksaw blade when sawing in tight corners. (Photo. Steve Williams)

type snips they have a double-fulcrum joint to give greater leverage, and the blades have fine serations to grip the metal.

A good quality hacksaw with a sturdy frame is essential. Don't forget, good quality does not necessarily mean new. Use different blades for different materials. Take advice when purchasing blades, and always fit them so that the cutting teeth face

Fig. 2.16. A selection of files. It is essential that a correctly fitting handle is used at all times. (Photo. Steve Williams)

the front or forward stroke. Obtain a wire-framed 'Junior' hacksaw, which is ideal for tight areas or small jobs.

Files are used to give a smooth finish, or for shaping by removing metal. They come in various lengths and shapes. The shape is the file's cross-section, which can be flat, square, triangular, round or half round. The teeth can be coarse or fine, or anything in between. A coarse or 'bastard cut' file will remove a lot of metal quickly but will leave a rough finish. A 'second cut' file will remove metal slowly and leave a smooth finish. The finest finish is achieved with a 'smooth cut' file. The pointed end of the file is called the tang, to which is fitted a handle which always used to be wooden but is now quite often plastic. **Never use a file without a handle**. Without one you are almost sure to stab your hand with the pointed tang.

Fig. 2.17. A special tool for smoothing and shaping glassfibre and metal. (Photo. Steve Williams)

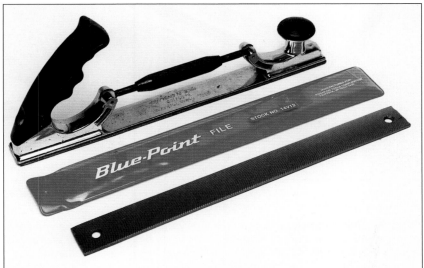

Fig. 2.18. A selection of hammers of different weights. The rubber face hammer is ideal for dressing aluminium panels. (Photo. Steve Williams)

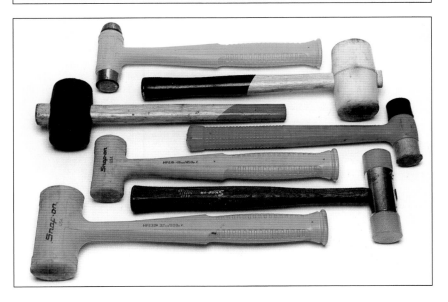

I never seem to have enough hammers, but a good 1lb (0.5kg) engineer's ball pein hammer will suffice. If you can afford it, a soft-faced hammer (either hard rubber, hide or nylon) will be most helpful, especially for dressing aluminium panels round the tubes of the space frame chassis.

Fig. 2.19. A selection of self-grip clamps for holding metal items together when welding. (Photo. Steve Williams)

Fig. 2.20. Blind holders and a pair of side-grip holders. With the special pliers, these are useful for holding metal parts before the final welding or pop riveting, and will not damage surfaces. (Photo. Steve Williams)

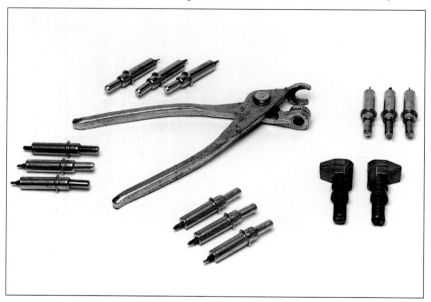

CLAMPING

Clamps come in a variety of types but all serve the same function of gripping two or more pieces of material together. The most common type is the G-cramp on which one adjustable face is moved by a screw thread. There are also lever locking clamps which come in several designs and sizes. The specialist ones tend to be a little expensive, but I have found that I can make my own by buying locking clamps with worn out jaws, then making my own jaws from scrap and welding them on. In this way you can obtain a full set of specialist welding clamps for a fraction of their cost new.

The ideal vice for work on your Locost project will have 5in (127mm) wide jaws. It will hold work safely when you are cutting, drilling, grinding and filing. You can also use it for clamping two pieces of metal together when

Fig. 2.21. Panel clips for securing metal sheets prior to riveting or welding. (Photo. Steve Williams)

welding, but remember not to let the heat get too close to the vice as this could damage it.

Secure your vice firmly, and remember that a vice is only as secure as the bench it is bolted to.

DRILLING AND GRINDING
An electric drill is the one power tool that is almost indispensable. Apart from making holes it can be used to power grinding stones, rotary wire brushes and various types of sanding and buffing accessories **(and don't forget to wear goggles when using it for these purposes)**.

A note of caution: if buying this tool second-hand, please have it

Fig. 2.22. Electric drill and angle grinder, with: 1. Sheet metal nibbler; 2. Stripping disc (for removal of light rust, paint, etc.); 3. Wire brush; 4. Cutting wheels; 5. Essential eye protection. (Photo. Steve Williams)

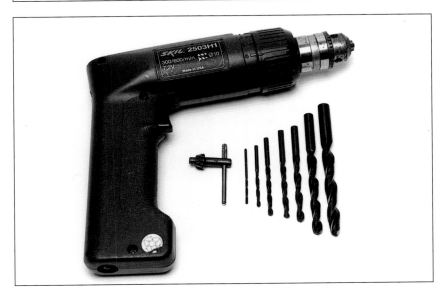

Fig. 2.23. A battery-operated rechargeable drill. Not essential if you have a mains-operated drill, but so light and compact to use. I was able to drill all the pop rivet holes to aluminium panel the chassis on one charge. (Photo. Steve Williams)

Fig. 2.24. A 4in (102mm) angle grinder and goggles. Never attempt to use a grinder without wearing goggles. (Photo. Steve Williams)

checked over by a qualified electrician. If the cable is frayed or damaged, or the plug wired incorrectly the results can be fatal.

If you do acquire an angle grinder it will probably be the most potentially dangerous tool in your kit, and as with the drill, if buying second-hand, do have it checked by a qualified electrician and **always wear goggles and protective clothing (including strong gloves) when using an angle grinder**. The three main attachments to it are grinding discs, cutting discs and sanding discs which are used in conjunction with a flexible plastic backing. Used with care, an angle grinder will save hours of work and will produce a professional finish to your metal. It can be used for dressing welds on the space-frame chassis where the area is to be panelled and you need a flat finish.

FIXING

A pop riveter is used to rivet materials together. It is particularly useful for joining dissimilar materials which cannot be welded, e.g. fixing the aluminium panels of your Locost to its steel frame. I also use mine to make temporary fastenings for body panels prior to welding, and then, if the fit is not quite accurate the rivets can be removed, the panel adjusted and refitted. It is worth buying a rivet gun with replaceable heads so that you are not restricted to one size.

On your Locost all the aluminium panels are secured with ⅛in (3mm) rivets. The other three most commonly used sizes are ³⁄₃₂in (2mm), ⁵⁄₃₂in (4mm) and ³⁄₁₆in (5mm) diameter. Rivets come in different lengths, but for our purpose we will use ⅜in (10mm) length.

Fig. 2.25. A hole puncher for use prior to riveting. (Photo. Steve Williams)

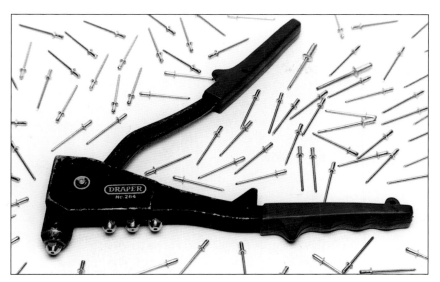

Fig. 2.26. A pop rivet gun and a selection of rivets. Note the four interchangeable heads. (Photo. Steve Williams)

Fig. 2.27. A Rivnut tool for setting threaded nuts in chassis tubes or panels. (Photo. Steve Williams)

WELDING EQUIPMENT

As explained in Chapter 1, there are three main methods of welding – gas, arc and MIG. I would advise a beginner to obtain MIG welding equipment for two main reasons. The first is cost, as nowadays inexpensive DIY MIG welders are available both new and second-hand. The materials are inexpensive, too, and – perhaps most important – with MIG a novice welder can produce first class results with minimal training.

An arc welder is cheaper to buy, but more difficult to master, especially on the material used to construct the Locost. The welding is more violent, less easy to control and more inclined to burn through or blow holes in the workpiece. Another problem is that the welds form a black slag which has to be chipped away with a special pointed hammer, making it a messy and time-consuming process.

The other of the three methods is gas welding, involving two gas cylinders, one of oxygen and one of acetylene, together with hoses, gauges, torches and a welding or bottle trolley. This is probably the most versatile method of all the equipment for it can be used for heating and cutting (useful for dismantling your donor vehicle, as a little heat will release the most stubborn rusted nuts), bending and shaping, welding and brazing. But I have found that it takes longer to teach novices to gas weld, and certainly a greater level of skill is required than in MIG welding. It is also slower and, because of the greater amount of local heat generated, one of the major problems is heat distortion, which could affect the accuracy of your chassis frame. Having said all that, the neatness of gas welding done by an expert is a joy to behold.

It is not possible to purchase the gas cylinders outright. Instead, you have have to enter into a rental agreement with the supplier, but it is possible to rent miniature cylinders (BOC Portapak). Although not aimed specifically at the novice or DIY market, they might help reduce costs and storage space. I think it would be fair to say, though, that this type of equipment is potentially more dangerous than the other forms of welding.

SAFE WORKSHOP PRACTICE

This is so important that I could fill a book just listing all the danger times and things to be aware of, but basically safety is down to just plain common sense. Think of your own safety, think of others and think the job through before you start.

Power tools and welding equipment present the greatest hazards. Make sure that all your electrical equipment is safe (including extension leads), and if in doubt have it checked by a qualified electrician. Flying sparks from angle grinders and swarf from drilling can cause terrible eye injuries. When using any grinding, drilling, buffing, polishing, cutting or shaping power tools wear safety

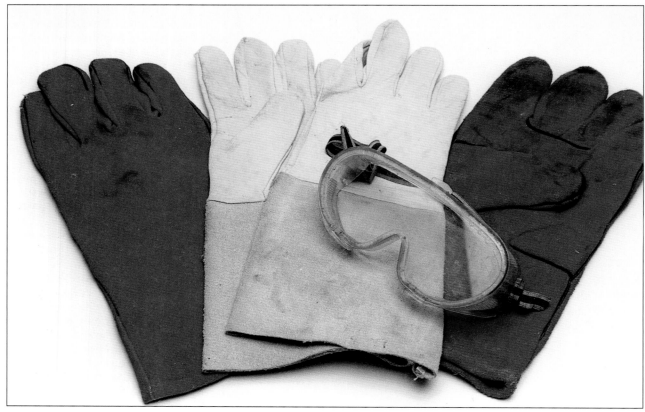

Fig. 2.28. Gauntlets and goggles. Essential for grinding and cutting operations. (Photo. Steve Williams)

goggles. Make sure the goggles are in good condition. If you can't see what you are doing and are working part blind, it produces yet another hazard. Make sure you have goggles for helpers and spectators, as sparks can travel up to 20ft (6m). For welding, have an adequate mask or goggles, and be aware that gas welding goggles are for gas welding and not for MIG or arc welding. For these you use full face masks. For any welding, wear protective clothing and gloves, making sure your arms are well covered. Keep all inflammable substances away from the workshop where you are welding or grinding.

Keep a clean and tidy workspace, and avoid trailing leads and cables as these constitute tripping hazards.

As your Locost takes shape it will need supporting at a safe and comfortable working height. Axle stands are ideal, but I also have several 18in (50cm) square wooden blocks which make firm supports. Do not be tempted to balance the project on bricks or boxes, as these may crumble or collapse.

Always keep a basic first-aid kit close by, and make sure other people know where it is. It also makes sense to have a fire extinguisher in your work area. One of the dry powder type suitable for electrical and liquid fires is ideal.

See also the welding safety precautions listed in Chapter 1.

PART 2

SOURCING WHAT YOU NEED

CHAPTER 3

Parts and materials

It is a sad fact that Britain's damp climate, plus the use of salt on the roads in winter, results in the majority of MoT failures being because of extensive body corrosion rather than mechanical shortcomings. Such failures are generally not worth repairing, as the restoration of corroded underbodies, sills, wings and wheel arches is time consuming, labour intensive and therefore very expensive. Consequently, it is possible to find discarded vehicles in scrapyards or at dismantlers that have nigh perfect mechanicals despite their rotten bodies. At the time of writing the first edition of this book (1996), the majority of these yards would collect a complete car, such as a Mk I or Mk II Ford Escort, free of charge, or pay the owner £25 if it was delivered to them. (The scrapyard would expect to recover between £100 and £150 from the sale of the major components, the remainder being crushed for scrap value.) So, in order to get your vehicle for £25, or thereabouts, you also need to purchase direct from the owner. How do you find the car you want?

First, go direct to the place responsible for it being scrapped – the MoT garage. Tell them you are looking for a scrap Mk I or Mk II Ford Escort. With luck, they may already know of one that has failed the test recently, and be able to put you in touch with the owner; or they may be prepared to let you know when the next one comes along.

If this doesn't bear fruit, the second stage is to advertise in your local shop or newsagent's window. A typical advert would read:

WANTED
Mk I or Mk II Ford Escort
MoT failure or unroadworthy
Fair price paid
Contact: *I. Wannacar*
Tel. No. 01234 567890

Fig. 3.1. A suitable donor car. This Ford Escort has good tyres and wheels and, having proved to be mechanically sound, it formed the basis for a Locost project.

Do not forget that the owner of this type of vehicle has probably been told by the scrapyard that it can be collected but no payment will be made, so your offer of £25 should not sound unreasonable. However, Escorts of this age are now not so plentiful as they were when this book was first published – largely because so many have already been bought by the growing number of Locost builders.

It is also worth following the small advertisements in your local newspapers. Ask your friends to pass the word around at work and generally keep your eyes open. My project car was obtained by noticing it in a front garden on my

way to work every day, and over a three month period it did not appear to move an inch. When I knocked on the front door to ask if it was for sale, the look of relief on the owner's mother's face spoke volumes. A figure of £25 was soon agreed, and the next day, with the aid of a friend and a trailer it was on its way to a new home. My car was the 1100cc estate version, the advantage in this case being that the later models came with wide 5½J sports wheels as standard, which I thought would look good on our sports car and would also improve the handling, road holding and braking. It took my son and myself just a weekend to remove the parts that we needed from our donor car.

WHAT YOU NEED FROM YOUR DONOR CAR

The following is the list of parts that you need to take from your donor car, and if you have not tackled this sort of dismantling job before, it is worth buying a copy of the Haynes Workshop Manual for the relevant Ford Escort. This will also be of help if you decide to overhaul any of the components, but keeping to the budget price means that there is not a lot of scope for this, and you need to ensure that, before buying the Escort, its engine, gearbox and back axle are in good running order. In our case we contented ourselves with overhauling just the braking and steering system.

Major items:
Engine (complete with carburettor, starter motor, water pump, inlet and exhaust manifolds, gearbox and clutch including mounting brackets)
Rear axle (complete with brake drums)
Propshaft and universal joints (must be single section type as used in the 1100 Escort)
Steering rack (including mounting clamps, track rods and swivel joints)
Wheels (including tyres and wheel nuts)

Radiator (including connecting hoses if in very good condition)
Master cylinder for brake system
Windscreen washer system
Heater and fan unit (capable of defrosting/demisting windscreen)
Exhaust pipe and silencer

Controls, cables and instruments:
Steering wheel
Clutch, brake and accelerator pedal assembly (including plastic 'top hat' bushes and pedal return springs)
Clutch cable
Speedometer cable
Choke cable
Handbrake lever (including mounting bracket)
Dashboard instrument cluster

Electrics:
Alternator
Battery (including cable and earth straps)
Wiring loom
Starter motor solenoid
Ignition coil
Distributor
Horn
Horn relay
Fuse box
Headlamp units (if round)
Flasher unit for indicators
Fuel tank sender unit
Brake-light switch

Sundries:
Seat belts (if in good condition)
Petrol filler cap
Hoses and clips (if in very good condition)
Accelerator cable
Fuel pipes and clips

What you will also need is an old tin bath to use as a cleaning tank, some old paint brushes and scrapers, a pair of rubber gloves and about two gallons of paraffin. You could use one of the proprietary cleaning fluids, such as *Jizer* or *Gunk*. We considered this but, although we agreed they may have been quicker, more efficient and would definitely not have left the slightly oily paraffin film, we could not afford them on our

budget. However, if you set your mind to it you can justify most things, and we decided that as the parts would have to be stored until the chassis was ready, the oily film was a bonus. As you clean off all the old grease and dirt from the engine and other parts that you remove from your donor car, you will find that they start looking almost new.

Once dried off, wrap the parts in plastic bags, label them and store them ready for use when you assemble your car. In the interests of safety, it is advisable not to reuse brake linings and pads, even though they may seem to have life left in them. In our case, we had already decided that all wearing braking and steering components would be replaced with new.

It was about this time that we decided to start a log listing all those parts in store and all those still to be obtained, together with photographs, drawings and notes. You also need to keep receipts for all purchases made, or at least records, for the purpose of registering your finished car (see the chapter on legal matters).

Steering rack
It is a good idea to replace with new the rubbers in the two steering rack mounting clamps, and be sure to examine the condition of the track rod ends – making sure that the rubber ball-joint covers are not damaged or perished. If they are, you will need to replace them. It is possible that your local MoT station would check them for you if you are not sure of their serviceability.

Also check the rubber bellows on the rack for damage and oil leaks. These can be replaced very cheaply.

Rear brakes
The components of the rear brake drum units from the donor Escort should be checked over, in particular for drum wear, the condition of the wheel cylinders, and fluid leaks; and it is worth taking the opportunity to fit new brake linings. Ensure that

everything operates freely when reassembled.

Radiator

Check that your radiator is in good condition, with no visible signs of damage or leaks.

Hold it up to a bright light and look directly through the gills. Quite often these become blocked with a mixture of oil, dirt and dust, which restricts the airflow through the radiator and hence its cooling efficiency. If it is blocked, soak the radiator in a bath of paraffin, or one of the proprietary engine degreasers, and then gently hose it through. This usually clears it.

You will probably want to repaint your radiator, and the best colour to use is matt black as this permits heat to dissipate more readily.

Exhaust pipe

Two types of exhaust system are fitted to the Escort – one with a silencer only and one with a silencer and expansion box. In each case the standard exhaust manifold can be used, but you will not need the expansion box.

Battery

Car batteries are hazardous items containing sulphuric acid and producing an inflammable gas which can be ignited by the smallest spark. I can recall two occasions when I have been in a workshop when a battery has exploded, sending lead shrapnel and acid in all directions. So, when you remove the battery from your donor car it is important to store it away from your workshop, and do not install it in your car until all welding and grinding is completed, and you really need it for testing the systems. As it is likely to be in store for some time a regular two or three weekly charge will keep it in good order. Charge the battery in a well-ventilated room, and always connect or disconnect the charger leads before switching on, or otherwise a spark here could ignite the gas. When handling batteries the 'No Smoking' rule must be adhered to.

If the battery earth is corroded, try pouring boiling water over it. This should clean it, but if in doubt replace it. The engine earthing point is usually all right.

Wiring loom

The positioning of the major electrical components in your Locost are the same as in the donor Escort, so you can reuse the Escort's wiring loom. Naturally you must first examine it for obvious signs of damage – chaffing, fraying, cracked or damaged insulation, etc. All the wires are colour coded, so by following the Escort wiring diagram and colour codes, it becomes easy to understand – certainly no more difficult than the London Underground maps.

Starter motor

The starter motor will need cleaning after removal from the donor vehicle. Check that the pinion is free to move, then lubricate sparingly with a thin oil. Also check the condition of the teeth on the pinion and replace it if any are chipped or broken.

PARTS YOU REQUIRE FROM ELSEWHERE

Other parts and materials, additional to those taken from the donor car, are as follows.

Parts from breakers/autojumbles or similar:

Front hub assemblies (left and right, including disc brakes and bottom swivels) from a Cortina Mk III, IV or V. (Bottom swivels from a Maxi can also be used.)

2 x track rod ends from a Ford Transit van (part No. TA298 if bought from A.P. Lockheed). These are for use as the top swivel joints in your front suspension. When buying them be sure that both are the same part number and are right-hand threaded, because when supplying a pair it would be usual (in their original use as track rod ends) to provide one left-hand thread and one right-hand thread

4 x coil-over shock absorbers

18 x 1½in (38mm) wide Metalastic bushes with 1in (25mm) o.d. and ⁷⁄₁₆in (11mm) i.d. as used in Triumph Heralds. (These are readily available from after-market specialist suppliers.)

Metalastic rubber exhaust mounting, called a cotton reel (the type normally fitted to the tail pipe of the Mini)

Windscreen wiper motor, wheel boxes and wiper arms from a Mini. (Note: Ideally two-speed, one of which must exceed 45 cycles per minute, and wiper arms must park out of the driver's line of sight.)

Windscreen washer system with a capacity in excess of 1 litre

Handbrake cable system from Austin Allegro

Steering column and attached ignition switch gear and steering lock from (if not from the donor car) a Vauxhall Nova or Ford Sierra

4 x Mini-type SVA (Single Vehical Approval)-compliant direction indicator lamps

2 x SVA-compliant side repeater lights

2 x SVA-compliant rear lights

2 x SVA-compliant headlight/sidelight units

An SVA-compliant rear red foglight

Back seating from the donor car

Electric fan

Ford Fiesta thermostat housing and temperature sender unit

Miscellaneous second-hand rocker switches (not toggle switches)

Front brakes

In sourcing the front hub assemblies it goes without saying that the components should be in good serviceable condition, the discs without heavy rust or corrosion (light surface rust is acceptable), and without surface damage or scoring. If an overhaul of these components is required, full details can be found in the Haynes Mk III, IV or V Cortina Workshop Manual. I would advise you to fit new disc pads.

Fig. 3.2. Front hub assembly as fitted to a Mark III, IV or V Cortina. (Photo. Steve Williams)

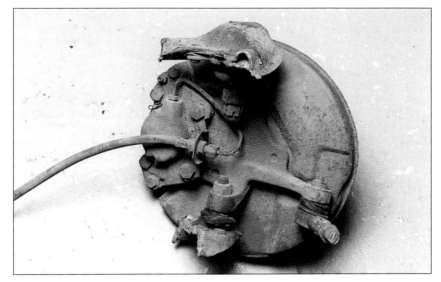

Fig. 3.3. Front hub assembly showing disc and caliper as fitted to a Mark III, IV or V Cortina. (Photo. Steve Williams)

Electric fan

The radiator fan on the Mk I or Mk II Escort donor car is belt driven, and as there won't be room for this in your Locost you will need to buy a second-hand electric fan. There are several types to be found in scrapyards, some standard factory fitments and some after-market alternatives. Some are designed to be fitted behind the radiator and some in front – a sucker or a blower. Try to obtain any wiring that goes with it.

Fig. 3.4. This electric fan cost £2 at an autojumble. Its origins are unknown, but it is beautifully made with a cast alloy surround and is very powerful.

Lights and indicators

It's necessary to make yourself fully aware of current vehicle lighting regulations, and whichever way you choose to interpret them with regard to the car you are building, keep in mind your ultimate need to get it through the Single Vehicle Approval test. To avoid disappointment, and in the interests of safety, the best route must surely be to fit lights that comply with current legislation and have the necessary approval markings. The *SVA Inspection Manual* sets out what is required, including siting and alignment, etc.

In addition to front and rear direction indicators, you must fit side repeaters on both sides of the car. Front position lamps can be incorporated in the headlights, and along with the rear position lamps, brake lights, reflectors, a number plate lamp and a rear red fog light must be fitted. Reversing lamps are optional, but if you do fit one (or two) then rulings must be followed.

Switches, knobs and levers

Legislation requires that all projections and sharp edges on interior fittings are kept to a minimum. This tends to rule out the old-style toggle switches, and the safe option is to use rocker switches. There is, though, an 'exempt area' which extends to a point outside the radius of the steering wheel. The inspector at the SVA test centre will check the radius of curvature of the gearknob and handbrake lever, as well as the bezels on dashboard instruments (problems here can usually be solved by 'sinking' your instruments into a deeply padded dashboard).

Windscreen wiper motor, washer and demister

On our original car the windscreen wiper motor, along with ancillary fittings and brackets, came from a Mini. The thing to bear in mind is that for test-passing purposes you will need a motor that is capable of driving the wipers at a speed in excess of 45 cycles per minute, and that parks the wipers out of the driver's line of view through the windscreen. To this end it's a good idea to use a two-speed wiper motor. For the narrow Locost windscreen, shorter blades will have to be obtained. If, instead of a windscreen, you fit an aero screen, no wipers or demisters will be required.

Your windscreen washer system must have a reservoir capacity in excess of 1 litre and, with the wipers going, should be capable of clearing the windscreen. Electrically operated systems will be expected to stand up to between three and five seconds of pressure against blocked washer nozzles.

With non-folding windscreens it is also a test requirement to have an effective means of demisting and, in severe weather conditions, defrosting the screen. This can be achieved by incorporating the

Fig. 3.5. A set of lights, including side direction repeaters, which comply with current lighting regulations. (Photo. Steve Williams)

Fig. 3.6. Rocker switches. Note that toggle switches (as shown on the right) are no longer acceptable and may cause your car to fail the SVA test. (Photo. Steve Williams)

heater/blower system from your donor car, or by purchasing a heated windscreen.

THE MATERIALS YOU WILL NEED (factory offcuts/sale stock/new):

RHS (rectangular hollow section) 16swg steel (1in x 1in/25mm x 25mm)

RHS 16swg steel (¾in x ¾in/19mm x 19mm)

RHS 16swg steel with a wall thickness of ⅛in (3mm) (2in x 2in/51mm x 51mm)

Round steel tube ¾in (19mm) x 16swg

Seamless steel tube with 1in (25mm) outside diameter and ¹³⁄₁₆in (21mm) inside diameter – 3ft (1m)

Seamless steel tube of ¾in (19mm) x 16swg – 30ft (9m)

Seamless steel tube of 1in (25mm) x 16swg – 9ft (2.75m)

Round stock 1in (25mm) bar – 6in (152mm)

Steel sheet (16swg)

Steel plate offcuts ⅛in (3mm) thick

Steel strip (1½in x ⅛in/41mm x 3mm)

Steel strip (1in x ⅛in/25mm x 3mm)

Steel strip (½in x ⅛in/13mm x 3mm)

Steel tube, rubber hose and hose clips to fit (for fuel tank)

Aluminium sheet (18swg)

Aluminium capping strip (1in/25mm wide)

Rubber strip (1in x ⅛in/25mm x 3mm) – 5ft (1.5m)

Kunifer brake pipe (new)

Brake pipe fittings (unions and brackets)

Flexible brake pipes (front for Mk III, IV or V Cortina and rear for Mk I or II Escort)

Front brake disc pads (new)

Rear brake linings (new)

Hardboard (8ft x 4ft x ¼in/2.5m x 1.25m x 6mm), foam rubber and vinyl for interior trim

Glassfibre materials (mat, resin, etc.) for making nose cone and mudguards

Matt black paint for radiator, etc.

Rust inhibiting paint for chassis

Etch primer paint for aluminium panels

Top coat paint for bodywork (about 3 litres)

Assortment of nuts, bolts, washers, self-tapping screws and clips

Nylock nuts

Aluminium pop rivets (500 x ⅜in/9mm long and ⅛in/3mm diameter)

Aluminium extrusion for windscreen surround

Laminated glass (cut to shape) for windscreen (or use an aero screen)

Silicone bath sealant

• (It may be possible to find a second-hand or slightly damaged nose cone and mudguards.)

SOURCING THE RHS TUBE

We found that we needed a work plan to ensure we made, sourced and purchased parts in some fairly logical order and, as the basis of the car is the chassis, on to which are bolted all the Escort bits, etc., it was decided to give early priority to sourcing the steel tube.

The Locost's chassis is a space-frame construction with triangulated tubes, which makes an incredibly light and strong structure, resistant to loads both in compression and tension. It is made from a number of short lengths of tube, with the longest stretches (four pieces) being 5ft (1.5m), which means you can use factory offcuts.

Over the years, I have noticed all the wonderful offcuts in the scrap bins of steel fabricators and engineering firms, so I knew where to go for our tube. Following the practice of some of the kit-car manufacturers, we decided to build our chassis of 1in x 1in (25mm x 25mm) RHS (Rectangular Hollow Section), ¾in x ¾in (19mm x 19mm) RHS and ¾in (19mm) round steel. The wall thickness of the RHS and round tubes should be 16swg. The 'swg' stands for 'standard wire gauge', a traditional standard for measuring not only the thickness of wire but also sheet steel and, in our case, the wall thickness of our tube. To help you identify it, 16swg is about ¹⁄₁₆in (1.6mm). The higher the number, the thinner the wall, e.g. 18swg is thinner than 16swg. In modern car bodies the thickness of the steel is about 20swg.

We are fortunate in that we live close to a town with a steel making

Fig. 3.7. 1in square and ¾in square rectangular hollow section (RHS) of 16swg gauge. It is easily cut with a hacksaw and is used to make most of the Locost space-frame chassis. (Photo. Steve Williams)

and engineering tradition and there are at least a dozen engineering companies and steel fabricators, all a source of offcuts. A search through your *Yellow Pages* will enable you to find such companies local to you. I advise a very polite and careful approach when requesting offcuts, and if you are refused it may be that they are mindful of safety and insurance regulations and do not allow visitors to rummage through scrap bins or skips. But, with a bit of luck you should be able to purchase all your steel quite reasonably.

A point worth mentioning is that if your tube is sourced from several places, ensure that it is all to the same specification. If, for example, you have heavier gauge tube on one side of your chassis than the other it will flex at a different rate and marginally unbalance the handling of the vehicle.

If you don't see yourself singing 'any old iron' round the metal merchants, you could purchase new standard lengths from your local steel stockholder.

AUTOJUMBLES

If you like car boot sales, flea markets and antique fairs, you will love autojumbles. They are advertised in all the regular specialist car magazines and papers such as *Practical Classics*, *Classic Car Weekly* and *Motor Sport*, etc. They are often held in association with a car show, but the

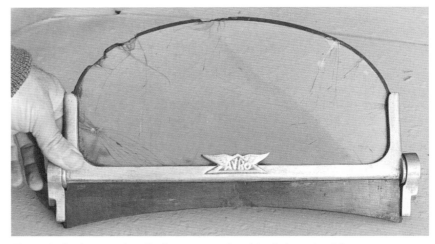

Fig. 3.8. An interesting find at an autojumble. I thought this aero screen might be suitable with a new piece of laminated glass cut and fitted. It cost a couple of pounds and I subsequently found it was a rare piece of aviation history, having come from a World War I Avro bi-plane fighter.

Fig. 3.9. Autojumbles offer a massive range of second-hand parts and equipment and, even if you don't find exactly what you are looking for, they represent an enjoyable day out amongst other car enthusiasts and meeting stall holders who are quite often prepared to look out for parts for you.

largest autojumble in this country is in the grounds of the National Motor Museum at Beaulieu held every summer over a weekend. There are about 2000 stands, and people say you can find anything for anything. The adjacent campsite has full facilities. I go every year with a group of friends, stay the weekend and have a great time. When we were building the first Locost I took my shopping list of wants, and by the end of the weekend had managed to tick everything off. Four coil-over fully adjustable shock absorbers for £60 (incidentally, the most expensive items for the whole project); a genuine but slightly damaged nose cone for £10; two damaged but repairable wings for £14, plus a great heap of light switches, brake pipe and petrol pipe, etc.

SCRAPYARDS

During the course of the original project I was a frequent visitor to local scrapyards and vehicle dismantlers. The difference between the two is that the dismantlers remove the parts, test and clean them and charge a fairly high price, whereas in a scrapyard you have to take the bits off yourself, pay your money and take your chance.

You will see that high up on the list of needs is aluminium sheet. I obtained ours from a commercial vehicle breaker's yard with the help of a pair of tin snips. I managed to cut the whole sides out of an accident damaged Luton box van, and this provided all the aluminium for panelling the chassis. It is an easy material to cut, work and shape and I was able to bring it home by rolling it into a 5ft diameter cylinder, securing it with string and putting it in a friend's van, all without denting or kinking

it. I suggest you obtain your material by similar means, but it is a good idea to have someone to help you. If the wind gets behind you when you are carrying a large sheet of metal you could well find yourself doing a bit of unscheduled hang-gliding!

The great incentive for all this work is that you can obtain all your 18swg aluminium for about £10 instead of £200, which is the price I was quoted for new standard sheets plus delivery and VAT.

The instruments for our original car came from a Triumph Dolomite Sprint which provided a speedo, rev counter, water temperature, oil pressure and fuel gauges and various warning lights. These instruments can be taken out still in

Fig. 3.10. This picture of the Ford sector in a scrapyard was taken for the first edition of this book in 1996, but with the growth in demand from Locost builders since then it is unlikely you will now find as many Mk II Escorts stacked up as you see here. Although government legislation has made scrapyards safer than they used to be, there is more chance of an accident whilst doing dismantling work in a scrapyard than in your own workshop. If you can afford it, most yards, for a small extra charge and deposit, will remove the parts for you.

Fig. 3.11. These are the sort of instruments that look best on a Locost. To comply with current SVA legislation concerning sharp-edged projections, it will be necessary to recess them in a padded dashboard. (Photo. Steve Williams)

the dashboard by removal of a few self-tapping screws, but be careful to trace all the wiring right back and unplug it from the loom. Do not be tempted to snip it off behind the instrument or the calibration may be upset.

There are many other vehicles which can provide instruments for your car, but try to obtain the separate round instruments found on older cars as they look so much better in our type of vehicle. An important point to watch is that some water temperature gauges are of the mercury type. These are easily identified by a long thin tube from instrument to cylinder head, wrapped in a sort of spring. If this tube is cut, broken or damaged in any way, the instrument is rendered useless. The same care must be taken with the oil pressure tube. These types of instruments are found on MG Midgets, Austin Healey Sprites and early MGBs.

The scrapyards also provided me with various switches, indicator lights, clips, screws, electric fan and Cortina hub, discs and calipers.

All the trimmed interior panels on the original car were cut from a damaged sheet of hardboard (it had been dropped on one corner) purchased from the local DIY shop. We stuck on ¼in (6mm) foam rubber, which was then covered in vinyl. I haggled for these in the local Sunday market. The gloss paint was obtained from a vehicle finish supply company who have an oddments counter with mismatched paint. I went every Saturday morning until I had found two tins of green, of different shades, and one tin of yellow. I mixed the two greens together to produce something close to British Racing Green and that gave us a really smart green and yellow sports car for a gloss paint cost of £7.50 instead of £60.

PART 3

MAKING
AND MODIFYING

CHAPTER 4

Making the space-frame chassis

The space-frame chassis is built from straight small diameter tubes. The design has full triangulation in all planes, and the advantage of this type of construction is that it combines lightness with great rigidity and strength.

This technique was used in the Second World War Wellington bombers, designed by Barnes Wallis, and it enabled them to sustain tremendous damage yet still keep flying, and after the war

Dr Ferdinand Porsche adopted the idea for his 1947 Cisitalia sports car. Colin Chapman's Lotus racing cars were designed with space-frames, and Maserati also used the method for its famous 'birdcage' racing car, so named because of its multitude of tubes. The smaller classes of open-wheeled racing cars are still of space-frame construction, as are several of the kit cars.

The design of our Locost chassis

is, therefore, not new, but we can relax in the knowledge that it is well tried and tested. However, its strength and integrity will only be as good as the accuracy of your construction and the quality of your welding. So, this is the most important part of building your car. Take great care with your measurements, and never feel ashamed at asking a qualified engineer and/or welder to check your work.

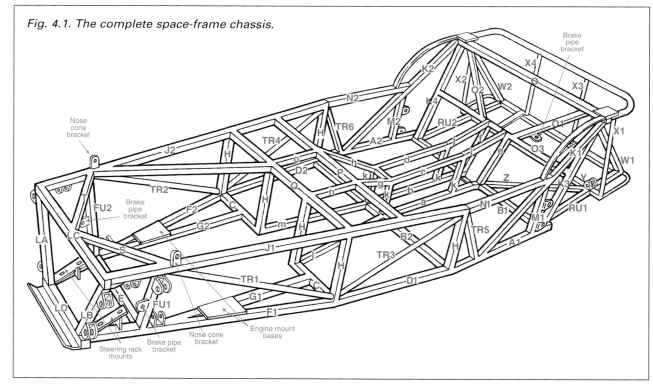

Fig. 4.1. The complete space-frame chassis.

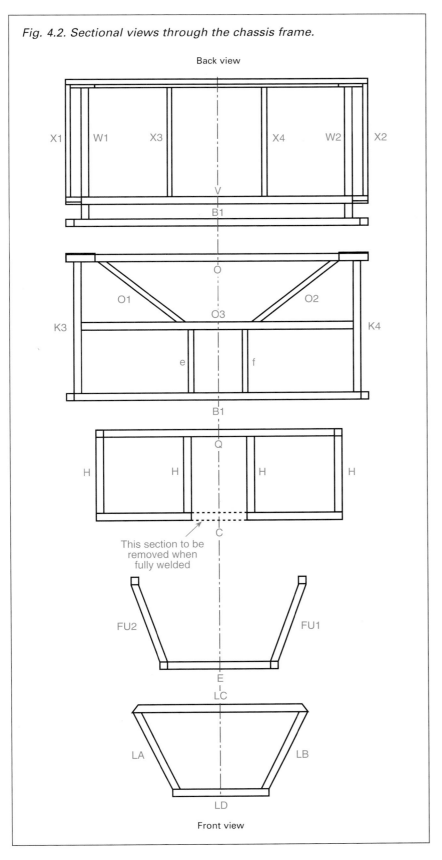

Fig. 4.2. Sectional views through the chassis frame.

Back view

Front view

The Locost gains additional strength from its secondary backbone chassis (formed by the transmission tunnel) and from a fully welded steel floor and front and rear panels. This serves also to ensure against any lozenging where transverse triangulation is not possible, such as the driver and passenger compartment.

WHAT YOU NEED

Lengths of 1in x 1in (25 x 25mm) 16swg RHS (rectangular hollow section) steel tube

Lengths of ¾in x ¾in (19 x 19mm) 16swg RHS steel tube

Lengths of ¾in (19mm) diameter 16swg round steel tube

52in x 42in (1321 x 1067mm) 16swg sheet steel (or roof of donor Escort)

⅛in x 1in (3mm x 25mm) steel strip

Various offcuts of 16swg sheet steel – about 4sq ft (1.25m²) in total

Various offcuts of ⅛in (3mm) steel plate for engine mountings, rear suspension, roll-over bar mountings and steering rack mountings. (3 pieces of 4in x 12in (102mm x 305mm) will suffice.)

Welding equipment and materials, with appropriate visor, gloves, etc.

CUTTING TO LENGTH

You can either cut your tube lengths piecemeal as you need them, or do all your cutting in one go. If you take the latter course it will be important to identify each length by marking it with a felt-tip pen (in any event it is a good idea to do this). Take care when cutting to ensure that the cut tube ends are square faced.

Using the 1in x 1in (25mm x 25mm) 16swg RHS steel tube cut and label the following lengths:

A1 and A2	32in (813mm) each
B1 and B2	40in (1016mm) each
C	32.4in (823mm)
D1 and D2	23in (584mm) each
E	15.1in (384mm)

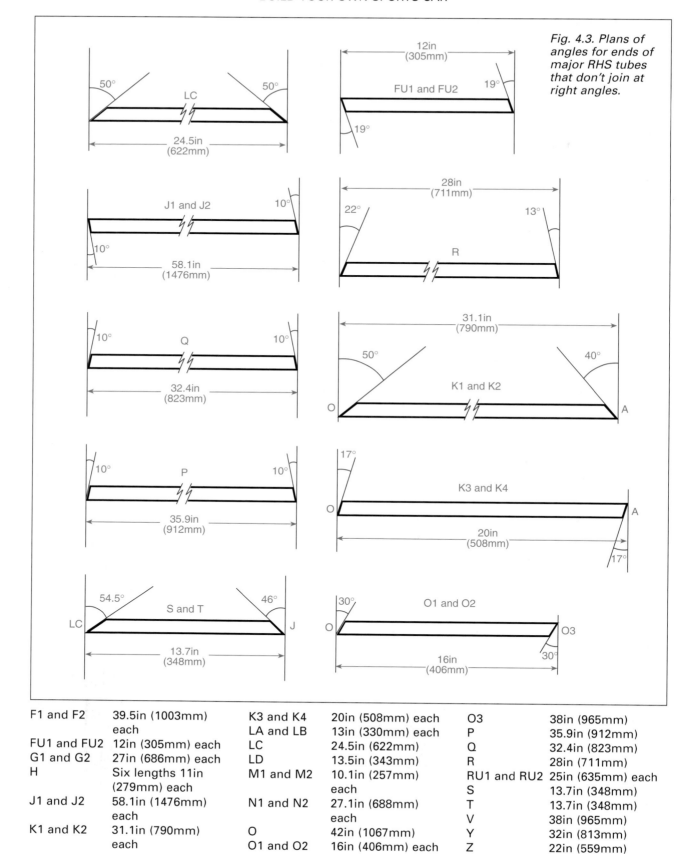

Fig. 4.3. Plans of angles for ends of major RHS tubes that don't join at right angles.

F1 and F2	39.5in (1003mm) each	K3 and K4	20in (508mm) each	O3	38in (965mm)
FU1 and FU2	12in (305mm) each	LA and LB	13in (330mm) each	P	35.9in (912mm)
G1 and G2	27in (686mm) each	LC	24.5in (622mm)	Q	32.4in (823mm)
H	Six lengths 11in (279mm) each	LD	13.5in (343mm)	R	28in (711mm)
		M1 and M2	10.1in (257mm) each	RU1 and RU2	25in (635mm) each
J1 and J2	58.1in (1476mm) each	N1 and N2	27.1in (688mm) each	S	13.7in (348mm)
				T	13.7in (348mm)
K1 and K2	31.1in (790mm) each	O	42in (1067mm)	V	38in (965mm)
		O1 and O2	16in (406mm) each	Y	32in (813mm)
				Z	22in (559mm)

Cut the following lengths from the ¾in x ¾in (19mm x 19mm) RHS:

TR5 and TR6	16.2in (411mm) each
W1 and W2	25in (635mm) each

Cut the following lengths from the ¾in x ¾in (19mm x 19mm) RHS for the transmission tunnel:

a and b	30in (762mm) each
c and d	5in (546mm) each
e and f	11.8in (300mm) each
g and h	4in (102mm) each
i and j	12.5in (317mm) each
k	4 lengths 8.5in (216mm)
l and m	21.5in (546mm) each
n and o	9in (229mm) each

Cut the following lengths from the ¾in (19mm) diameter round tube:

TR1	29.1in (739mm)
TR2	29.1in (739mm)
TR3	24.2in (615mm)
TR4	24.2in (615mm)
X1 and X2	18.9in (480mm) each
X3 and X4	16.8in (427mm) each
Tube to form luggage area	66in (1676mm)

Note

To be sure of an accurate fit, a slight angle will have to be filed (with a good coarse file) on the ends of some of the tubes, but if you check the plan and redraw the relevant portions to full size before cutting the tubes, you should be able to see the angles you need to cut them at, leaving just minimal filing for truing up during assembly.

PUTTING THE PIECES TOGETHER

Stage 1

The chassis is built without the need for a jig, but it is absolutely essential that you have a really flat surface to start from. I have found from experience that very few concrete garage floors are truly level, but this can be overcome by using an 8ft x 4ft (2.5m x 1.25m) sheet of ½in (13mm) block board. This will be sufficiently rigid, despite being laid on an uneven floor, to give you the flat surface you need.

Having got your flat surface, you must first mark on it (lengthways) the centre line with a fine marker pen. If you have to mark on a concrete floor, take great care to ensure that your line is a fine one and will be fairly permanent. If you use chalk, for example, you will find it difficult to obtain a line less than ¼in (6mm) thick, and the edges will tend to smudge, which could lead to errors when assembling. It is preferable to mark your lines with a coloured crayon. Taking your measurements from the scale plan, and using your centre line, now mark out the positions for the tubes. Check your right-angles with a set-square to ensure they are accurate.

First lay out tubes A1 and A2 and B1 and B2. The outside measurement of the rectangle they form should be 42in (1067mm) wide by 32in (813mm) long. When satisfied with the accuracy of your angles, tack weld all four tubes together.

Now position tube C on its mark, and then tubes D1 and D2, and when satisfied with your accuracy and the general fit, tack weld in place.

Following the same procedure, fit tubes F1, F2 and E and tack weld in place. Double check that the distance between the ends of F1 and F2 (at the front of the chassis) is 8.5in (216mm). Now fit tubes G1 and G2 (checking the 7in (178mm) distances along tube C between FI and GI and F2 and G2) and tack weld.

Special note

The position of tubes G1 and G2 on tube C can be altered to suit different engine installations. The distance between F1 and G1 along tube C for a 1100, 1300 or 1600cc Ford crossflow engine should be 5in (127mm). On engines which have the starter motor on the offside, G2 may have to be moved

Fig. 4.4. One Locost builder's way of achieving the necessary flat surface for laying out the bottom rails of the chassis.

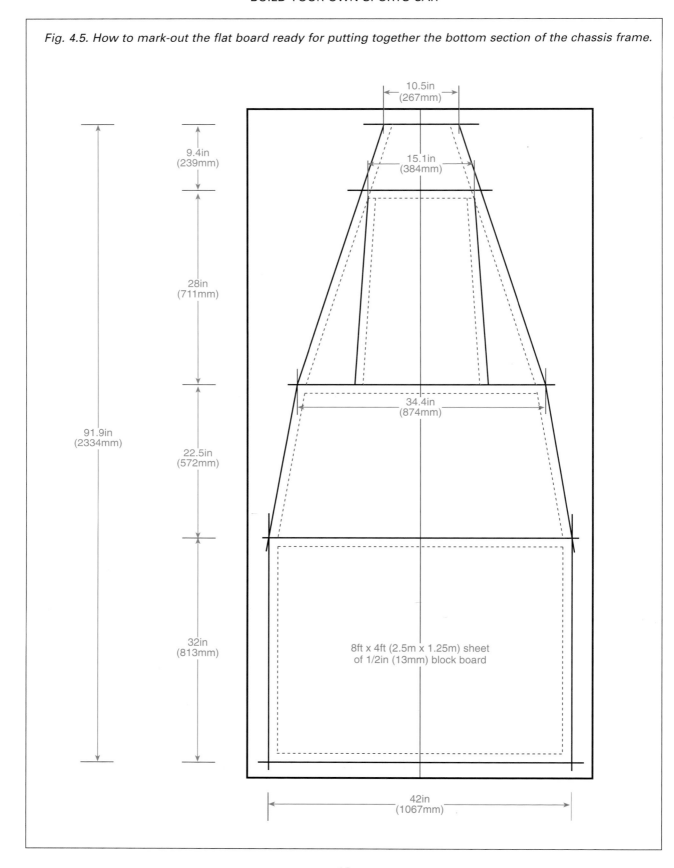

Fig. 4.5. How to mark-out the flat board ready for putting together the bottom section of the chassis frame.

8ft x 4ft (2.5m x 1.25m) sheet
of 1/2in (13mm) block board

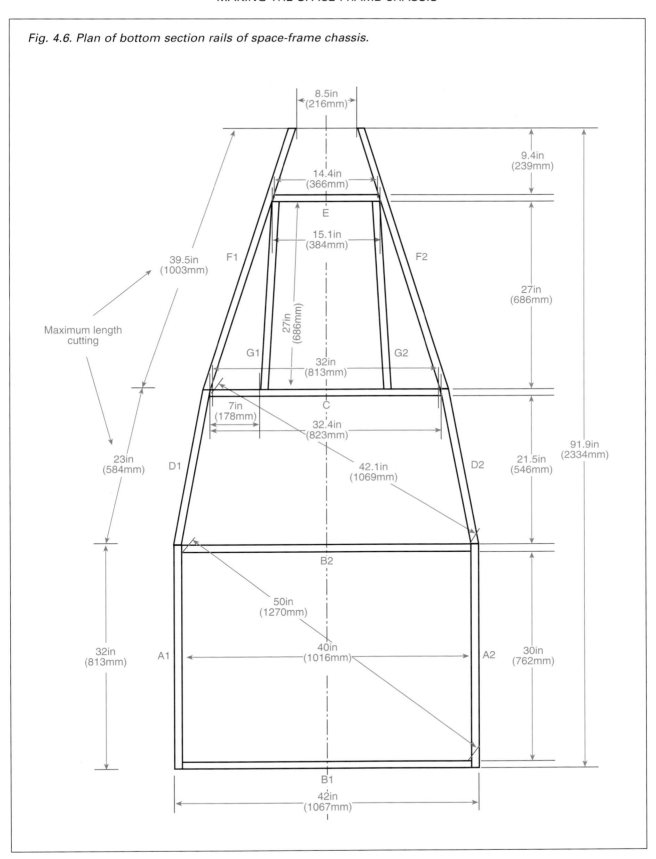

Fig. 4.6. Plan of bottom section rails of space-frame chassis.

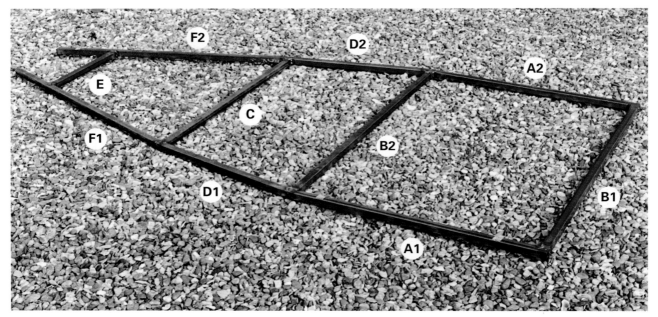

Fig. 4.7. The first stage of the chassis. Ten pieces of 1in x 1in (25mm x 25mm) RHS welded together.

over. To be certain of adequate clearance if any other engine is fitted, it is best to stand your chosen engine and gearbox on your flat build surface in the correct position between G1 and G2 and make any adjustments necessary.

Now that all the tubes in Stage 1 have been tack welded, mark (using a felt tip pen) TOP on two or three tubes, so that if you have had to move G1 or G2 you will be able

to identify the right side up when you start building the rest of the chassis. One of my students, who altered these tubes to fit a BMC A series engine, didn't notice that he had started to build up on the wrong side until after reaching the painted rolling chassis stage, and having spent several hours trying to work out why his engine would not fit, the truth dawned. Be warned!

Turn your tack-welded frame over and tack weld all the underside joints. File or grind flat your welds to be sure the chassis still sits level, and turn it back so that the top faces uppermost.

Stage 2

Take the four 11in (279mm) lengths of RHS marked 'H' and tack weld each in a vertical position (at right angles to the base) at either end of tube C and tube B2 (see plan and photograph). Use a set square to check their perpendicularity on both planes.

Next (following the plan measurements) construct assembly L from tubes LA, LB, LC and LD, shaping the necessary angles at the ends of the tubes. Note that whilst LD (13½in/343mm) will be tack welded to the ends of tubes F1 and F2 at the front of the chassis and will sit flat on the level building surface, LC is set back, meaning that LA and LB slope rearward when viewed from the side (see plan and photograph). When correctly aligned, tack weld together, and then tack weld assembly to F1 and F2, confirming that LC is 13in (330mm) above the flat building surface.

You now tack weld tubes JI and

Fig. 4.8. Positioning an engine and gearbox over the chassis frame to see what chassis modifications may be necessary to ensure it all fits into the finished job.

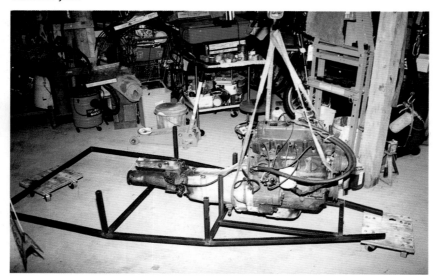

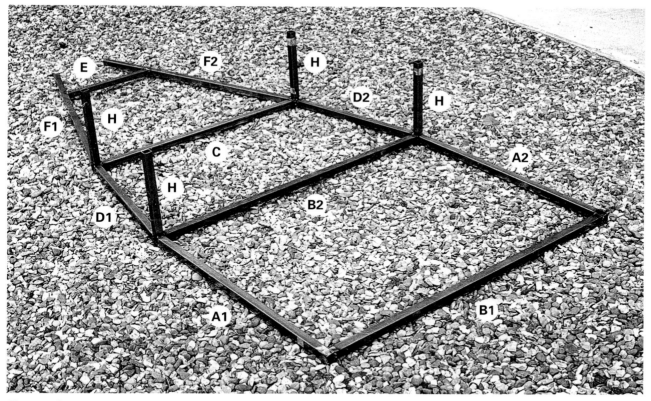

Fig. 4.9. Second stage of chassis construction. Four 11in (279mm) tubes at right angles to the base.

J2 (58.1in/1476mm) to the top of the upright 11in (279mm) H tubes (on each side of your chassis), linking them longitudinally with tube LC at the front of the chassis.

Tubes K1 and K2 are the next to fit, and care needs to be taken here

to set them at the correct angle. They connect to tubes A1 and A2 respectively, about 19in (483mm) from their B1 end, and should be

tack welded in place at an angle of 40° so that the other ends of K1 and K2 are 21in (533mm) from the flat building surface.

Fig. 4.11. The front chassis member (assembly L) clamped to a wooden jig to ensure the correct angle. The top tube should be set back 3in (76mm) from the bottom tube.

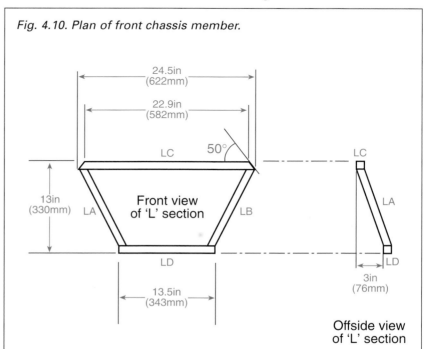

Fig. 4.10. Plan of front chassis member.

Front view of 'L' section

Offside view of 'L' section

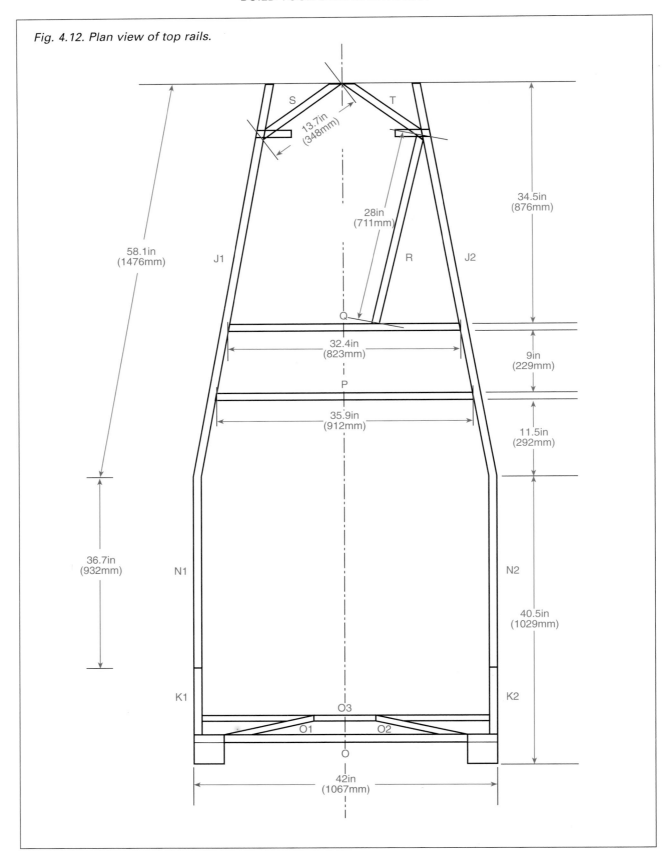

Fig. 4.12. Plan view of top rails.

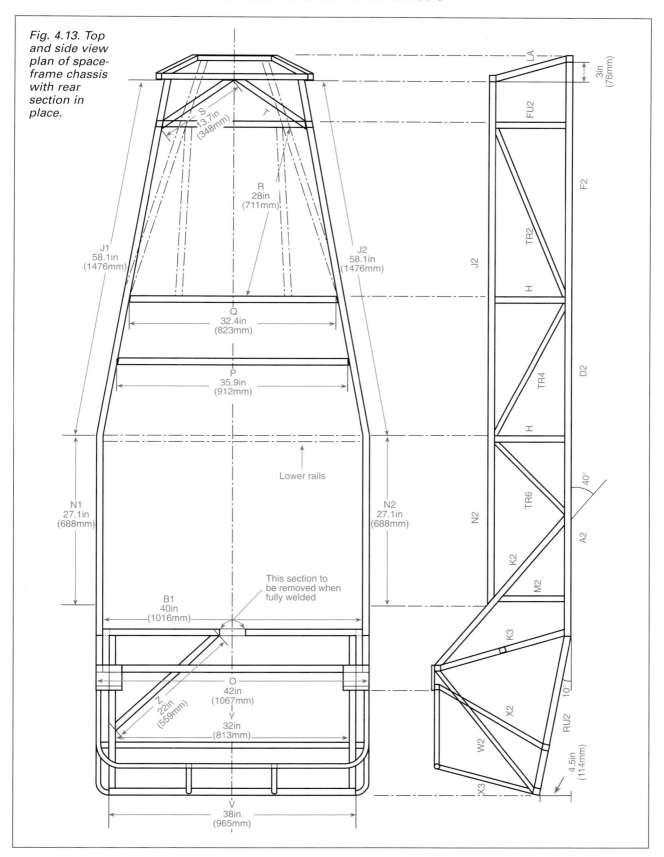

Fig. 4.13. Top and side view plan of space-frame chassis with rear section in place.

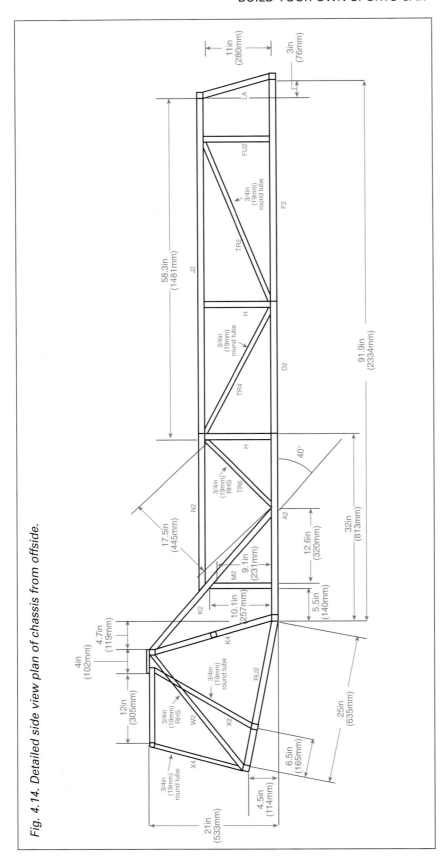

Fig. 4.14. Detailed side view plan of chassis from offside.

Now fit tubes M1 and M2 (10.1in/257mm). These are perpendicular supports between A1 and A2 and K1 and K2 respectively and their fixing point to A1 and A2 is 6.5in (165mm) along from B1. Recheck K1 and K2 for correct height and angle and, when satisfied all is well, tack weld in place.

Tubes K3 and K4 can now be tack welded in position between the ends of B1 and K1 and B1 and K2, followed by tubes N1 and N2 (27.1in/688mm) which should be level with and butt up against the ends of J1 and J2 (13in (330mm) above the level building surface) linking the rear H uprights with K1 and K2. Tube O (42in/1067mm) can now be tack welded between the tops of K1 and K3.

The next tubes to fit are P (35.9in/912mm) and Q (32.4in/ 823mm). These are cross-members between J1 and J2. Tube Q is fitted where the two front uprights (H) connect to J1 and J2, and tube P fits 9in (229mm) back from this. R (28in/711mm), S (13.7in/348mm) and T (13.7in/ 348mm), suitably angled (see plan), are then tack welded in place. Your chassis is now beginning to take shape.

Now separately tack weld RU1 and RU2 (25in/635mm) to V (38in/965mm) on your flat building surface. The other ends of RU1 and RU2 are tack welded to B1, but at an angle. The correct angle can be achieved by putting a 4.5in (114mm) block under V before welding RU1 and RU2 to B1 or by cutting the ends of RU1 and RU2 on a 10° angle. Alternatively, if you tack weld on the upper side only it will be possible to bend (or hinge) these tubes to the correct angle before the final weld.

Now cut out two 4in x 4in x ⅛in (102mm x 102mm x 3mm) steel plates, and along one edge of each weld a 4in (102mm) length of ¾in x ¾in (19mm x 19mm) 16swg RHS steel tube. The opposite edges of both plates are then welded in position on tube O (see plan) so that they are horizontal.

Fig. 4.15. Chassis top rails in place.

Cut tubes W1 and W2 from 1in (25mm) RHS to fit, as shown in drawing, and fully weld in place.

The next tube to fit is Y (32in/813mm). This fits parallel to and 6.5in (165mm) in front of tube V, straddling RU1 and RU2. This tube is the forward support for the fuel tank, and if necessary it can be moved further forward to make room for a larger tank, but if you do decide to reposition tube Y make sure you allow ample clearance for the Panhard rod and rear axle. In the position shown it supports a tank holding about 35 litres.

Round tubes X1 and X2 can now be welded in position between the extensions to each end of tube Y (see *Fig. 4.13*) and the ¾in (19mm) sq. tube on the underside of the 4in x 4in (102mm x 102mm) steel plates attached to tube O. Then fit tube Z (22in/559mm), with suitably angled ends, between B1 and U2. This is the Panhard rod support tube.

The only lengths of tube needing to be bent are the top rear tube that forms the luggage area and two short tubes at the bottom left and right of the rear assembly. These are made from ¾in (19mm) round steel so that the rear aluminium panel can be rolled round them neatly. A helpful plumber would most likely be able to bend these

for you with a special pipe-bending tool, but you can do it yourself in a vice – bending a little, then moving the tube, and bending a little more, and so on. Any kinks that form will be on the inside edge and will

Fig. 4.16. At this stage the chassis will weigh about 35lb. (Photo. Steve Williams)

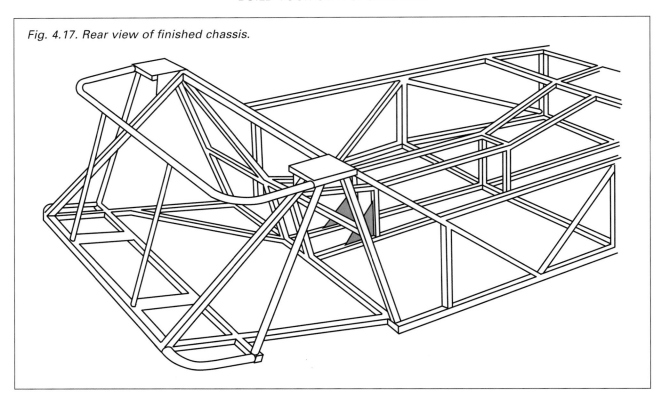

Fig. 4.17. Rear view of finished chassis.

eventually be covered by the aluminium sheet.

As you will see from the plan, I made the opening 12in (305mm) deep. This is because it gives an attractive angle to the rear panel, but if you want a larger luggage space there is no reason why you shouldn't extend the opening up to the point of having the rear panel almost vertical.

Round tubes X3 and X4 should now be welded in place between the top luggage area tube and tube V. These are positioned vertically, 6in (152mm) each side of the centre line. If you intend to carry a spare wheel on the rear panel, a strip of mild steel ⅛in (3mm) thick by 2in (51mm) wide welded between X3 and X4 will provide a rigid fixing to take the weight. Note fuel tank supports in *Fig. 4.17*.

Stage 3

The transmission tunnel is made from ¾in x ¾in (19mm x 19mm) RHS steel tube, and the plans are for an 1100cc or 1300cc Ford Escort gearbox. If other transmissions are fitted, the tunnel can be adjusted to suit. On my son's car we fitted a

BMC gearbox and the tunnel had to be widened on the passenger side, which reduced the passenger footwell. I think it best to avoid any engine/gearbox combinations which reduce the width of the driver's footwell as the control pedals need the correct area for safety and comfort.

Follow the plans and photographs, in particular *Figs. 4.1, 4.18* and *4.19*, for fitting the transmission tunnel rails – making allowances for the needs of your choice of engine/gearbox. Once the positioning of rails l and m has been established, weld in the two final (of a total of six) H upright rails, linking rails C and Q, and then the centre section can be cut from main rail C. At the same time the centre of main rail B1 can be cut out and moved forward to allow room at the rear end of the transmission tunnel for the differential on the back axle. Remember to cap all open ends of chassis rails to prevent wet and mud getting in and causing rust and corrosion.

At this stage your chassis will be looking fairly much like a sports

car, and most people I know cannot resist the temptation to sit in and try it for size. Even though it is only tack welded, you will be surprised at how rigid and strong your chassis is. But, before you weld it up fully, check all the dimensions and angles for accuracy, particularly when viewed from front and rear. Someone with a 'good eye' should be able to spot any irregularity. If there are some small errors it won't be the end of the world, as the tack welds can be ground off and any tubes replaced or repositioned.

Once you are happy with things, you can proceed to fully weld the whole chassis. It is best to weld alternately from one side to the other. You will notice that, with the exception of the Panhard rod support tube (Z), joints are identical on each side, and if you weld them in sequence it will help to avoid any heat distortion. You must be very thorough and make sure you have not missed a weld. Turn the chassis upside down and on its sides, inspecting all the joints.

When satisfied, weld in the four ¾in (19mm) round tubes TR1, TR2,

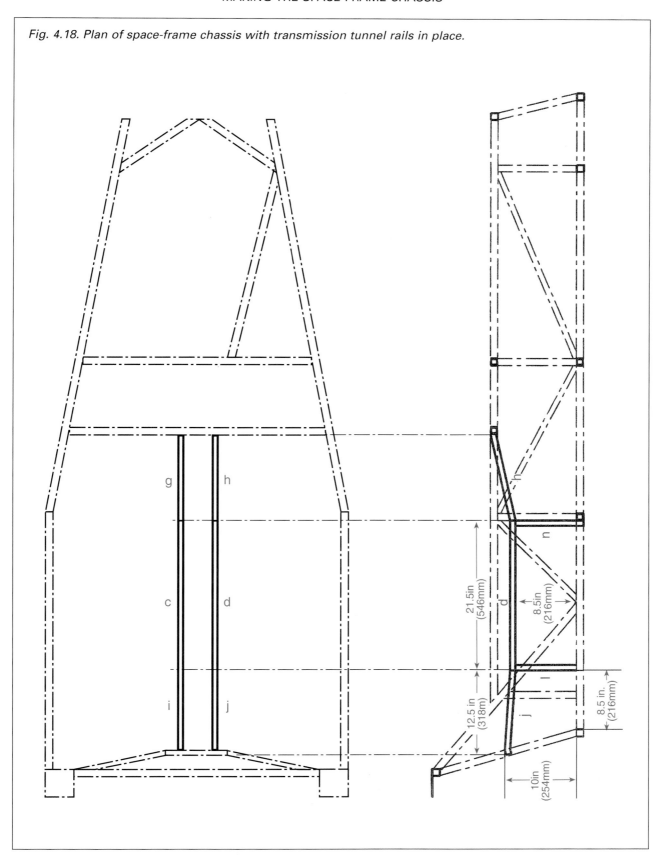

Fig. 4.18. Plan of space-frame chassis with transmission tunnel rails in place.

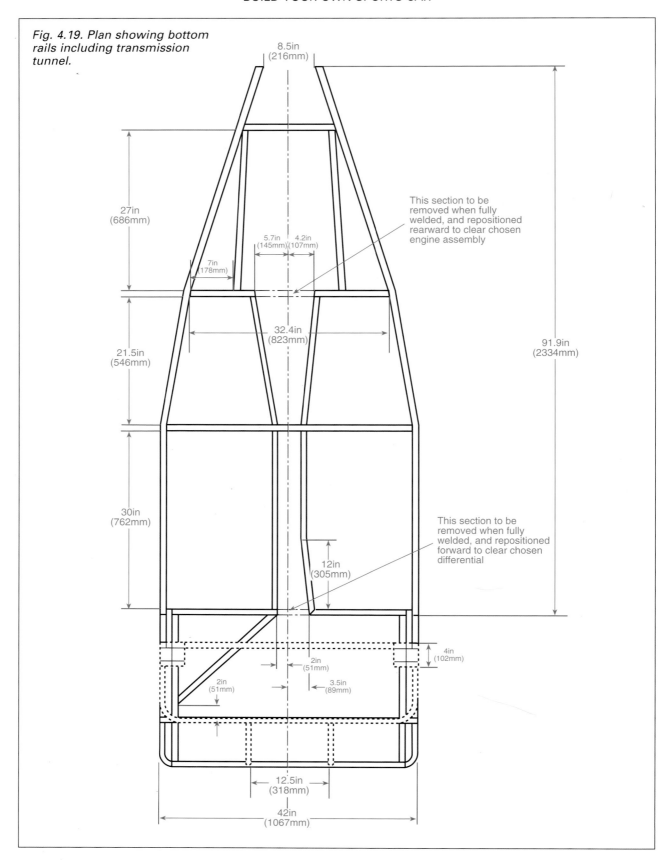

Fig. 4.19. Plan showing bottom rails including transmission tunnel.

Fig. 4.20. Rear view of main chassis with transmission tunnel welded in place.

TR3 and TR4, and the two ¾in (19mm) square tubes TR5 and TR6.

When the chassis is fully welded, a centre section of tube C needs to be cut out to make room for the gearbox. Also cut out the centre section of tube B1 to allow clearance for the differential flange. Cap the open ends by welding on 1in (25mm) squares of 16swg mild steel.

Fig. 4.21. Front view of main chassis with transmission tunnel welded in place.

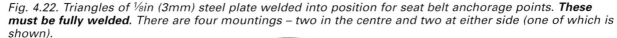

Fig. 4.22. Triangles of ⅛in (3mm) steel plate welded into position for seat belt anchorage points. **These must be fully welded.** There are four mountings – two in the centre and two at either side (one of which is shown).

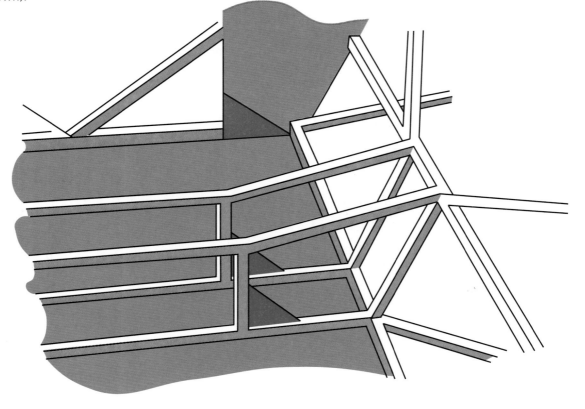

Fig. 4.23. An SVA-compliant upper anchorage point for a diagonal type seat belt. This is attached to a triangular steel plate welded on to the roll bar.

Fig. 4.24. A version of rear mountings for harness-type seat belt (seen from behind). These were given extra strength by welding in solid steel bars to connect rail O with rails O1 and O2 (as shown). A short length of RHS with a suitable nut welded into one end was then slipped over the upper part of the bar and welded in place. The threaded seat belt eye was then screwed into the nut.

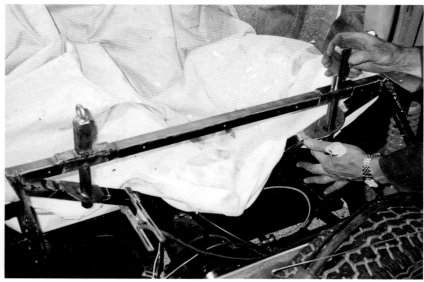

Fig. 4.25. The finished job. An SVA-compliant upper anchorage for a harness-type seat belt. (Photo. Steve Williams)

Seat belt mountings

These are made from 3in (76mm) triangles of ⅛in (3mm) steel plate and are fully welded in position in the chassis as shown in *Fig. 4.22*. These are suitable for lap and diagonal belts, but for racing type four-point belts, additional mountings can be made from ³⁄₁₆in (5mm) steel plate and welded to the chassis top rail (behind the seat back). To comply with regulations, these need to be raised above the chassis rail as shown.

Handbrake mountings

Two strips of ¾in x ⅛in (19mm x 3mm) offcuts can be welded between the top rails of the transmission tunnel so that, when bolted in place, the Escort handbrake (in both the on and off positions) allows the gearstick full travel, and is in a position to suit your preference.

Pedal cross-shaft mounts

Great care must be taken that the brake pedal length is enough to create sufficient leverage to

operate the master cylinder easily, and that sufficient clearance is left for the steering column.

Dismantle the pedal box from your Escort donor car by removing the clip and withdrawing the pivot shaft, taking care not to lose the plastic top hat bushes. With the

brake and clutch pedal (the bushes removed from the pedal box) reassemble on to the pivot shaft and sit in the chassis with some support behind your back (to simulate the thickness of a seat) and observe where your feet come. This will dictate the position of the pedals. It is also worth getting a helper to mark this position, then with your heel on the floor, measure the height to the ball of your foot and offer up the pedals to a comfortable position. You may find that the pedal pads are below the level of the ball of your foot, and that raising the whole assembly leaves insufficient clearance for the steering column. If this is the case, the pedals may be shortened by a couple of inches by cutting a piece off at the lower end and re-welding, not forgetting to remove the plastic bushes and the pedal rubbers which otherwise would be heat damaged. Offer back into the chassis again and, if the position is satisfactory, fabricate two brackets from ³⁄₁₆in x 1.5in (5mm x 38mm) flat steel for either end of the pivot shaft, then weld in place to the 1in x 1in (25mm x 25mm) RHS tube above the bulkhead.

Steering rack mounts

For the steering rack mounts refer

Fig. 4.26. Pedal cross-shaft mounts welded in position.

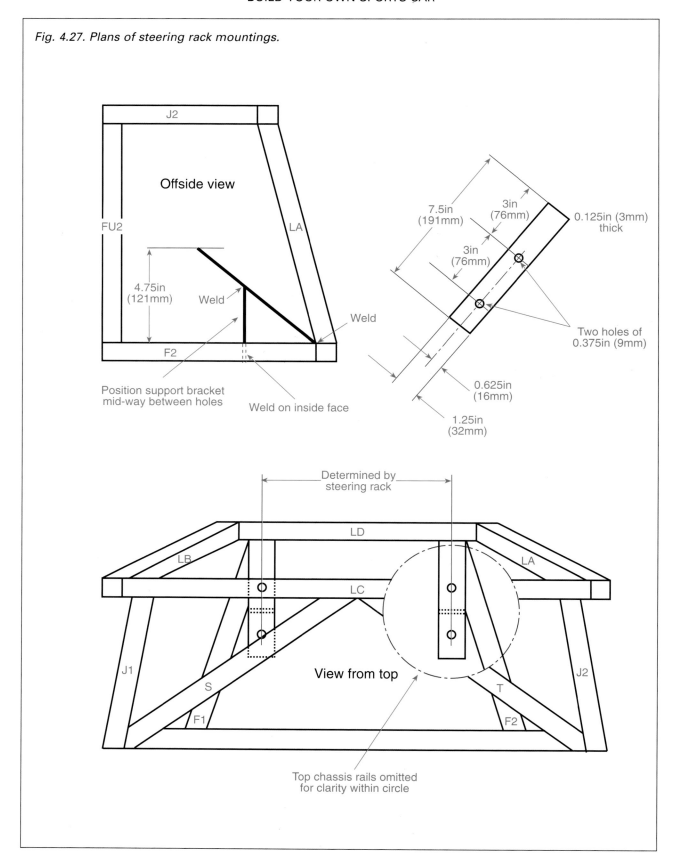

Fig. 4.27. Plans of steering rack mountings.

Offside view

J2

FU2

LA

4.75in
(121mm)

Weld

Weld

F2

Position support bracket
mid-way between holes

Weld on inside face

7.5in
(191mm)

3in
(76mm)

3in
(76mm)

0.125in (3mm)
thick

Two holes of
0.375in (9mm)

0.625in
(16mm)

1.25in
(32mm)

Determined by
steering rack

LD

LB

LA

LC

J1

S

F1

View from top

T

J2

F2

Top chassis rails omitted
for clarity within circle

Fig. 4.28. Front of chassis showing steering rack mounts, radiator mounts and nose cone bottom support panel.

to the plan and cut two strips of ⅛in (3mm) metal, and in each drill two holes corresponding to the

diameter and distance apart of the holes in the Escort steering rack clamps. Ensuring the rubbers are in

Fig. 4.29. Side view of steering rack and radiator mounts.

position, bolt the two strips to the steering rack, align and weld. Remove the steering rack and fabricate from scrap ⅛in (3mm) steel plate two steering rack mounting supports, and weld them vertically between the mountings and bottom chassis rails. Refit the steering rack to check for correct alignment.

Radiator mounting brackets
The radiator needs to be positioned at an angle for two reasons. One is to allow it to fit within the nose cone, and the other is to allow clearance for the hoses.

Fabricate the radiator mounting brackets from ⅛in (3mm) scrap steel to the desired shape, then tack weld in position on the front of the chassis (see *Figs. 4.28 and 4.29*). Bolt on the radiator and check for sufficient clearance for top and bottom hoses and trial fit the nose cone. Adjust as necessary and, when satisfied with the fit, remove the radiator and fully weld. I used the four radiator mounting bolts to also mount the electric fan and the horn.

Nose cone bracket

If you already have your nose cone, fit it to the chassis, checking that it is perfectly aligned, and from 16swg sheet steel make some brackets to secure it to the chassis in the correct position – two either side at the top and one in the centre at the bottom.

Roll-over bar

If you decide to fit a roll bar to your car, cut out two more 4in (102mm) square plates from ⅛in (3mm) thick steel, and drill four holes – one at each corner – in each plate. Position the plates on top of the 4in (102mm) square plates on the chassis at each end of RHS tube O, and drill holes through these in the same positions. Now fabricate a bow of round steel tube to suit the width of your car, i.e. the distance between the two plates at the ends of RHS tube O. Angle the ends of the round tube so that they sit flat on the plates, and weld on the two new plates that you have made. The finished bar can now be bolted, with high tensile bolts, to the chassis plates. To complete the

Fig. 4.30. An American builder's roll bar fitted in the way described here.

job, weld on two supporting struts connecting the roll bar to the points on the rear tube where the round tubes X3 and X4 connect. You don't *have* to fit a roll bar for road use, but it is a requirement for racing (see Chapter 20).

Suspension mounting brackets

Make 26 mounting brackets from ⅛in (3mm) mild steel strip 1.6in (40mm) wide. Each bracket needs a length of 4.55in (116mm) (see *Fig. 4.31*). These are the suspension mounting brackets.

Take a top and bottom wishbone and four suspension brackets, and assemble brackets on to wishbones. Carefully following *Fig. 4.33*, offer up the brackets in their correct position on the chassis. (Here a second pair of hands is

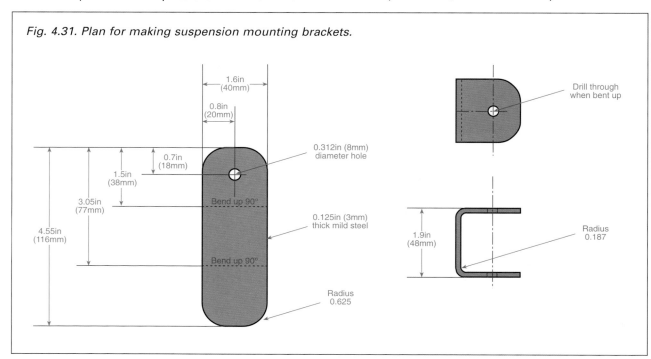

Fig. 4.31. Plan for making suspension mounting brackets.

Fig. 4.32. Mounting brackets formed from ⅛in (3mm) steel strip. (Photo. Steve Williams)

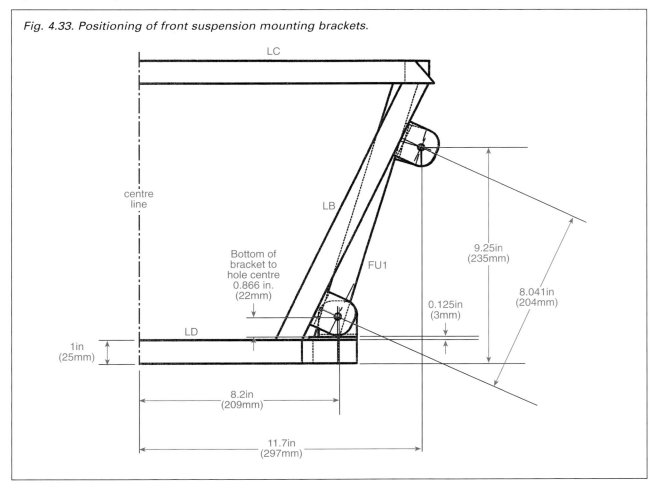

Fig. 4.33. Positioning of front suspension mounting brackets.

Fig. 4.34. Offside front suspension brackets welded into place.

essential, but make sure your helper has adequate eye protection.) You must be sure that both wishbones are parallel to the centre-line of the chassis and that they are also on a horizontal plane with the chassis.

Tack weld when you are satisfied with the positioning. It is essential you only tack weld, or heat may damage the rubber bushes in the wishbones. Recheck your measurements with the plan and, if everything is correct, withdraw the suspension bolts. Remove the wishbones and fully weld the brackets in place. When the weld has cooled, refit the wishbones and check for smooth up and down movement, remembering that on the road the movement is only two or three inches, depending on the type of springs and shock absorbers fitted. Repeat this process for the opposite side.

The rear suspension brackets are welded in position as shown in *Fig. 4.35*. It is advisable to support the

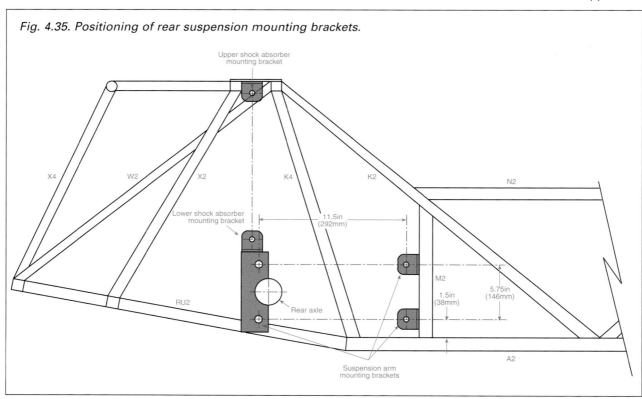

Fig. 4.35. Positioning of rear suspension mounting brackets.

chassis on axle stands, then place the axle in position and support it at the correct height, with the four trailing arms fitted and parallel to the chassis. In order to weld the Panhard rod mounting to the chassis in the correct position, fit the Panhard rod to the axle, bolt a suspension bracket to the free end and, ensuring the axle is perfectly central in the chassis, tack weld the bracket in place – then remove the Panhard rod and fully weld. An alternative method is to locate the axle in the correct position, weld in the chassis bracket and make the Panhard rod to fit between the two mountings.

Weld the suspension brackets in position, making sure that the top mountings are in line with the bottom wishbone shock absorber mountings and that the rear shock absorber top mountings are in line and above the axle bottom shock absorber mountings.

Stage 4

All that remains now is to panel in the floor with 16swg sheet steel. On my son's car we salvaged the central roof section from the donor Escort. After we removed the paint with a sander, we stood the chassis on the sheet, marked round the edge of the chassis with a scriber and cut out what we needed with tin snips.

The chassis then needs to be turned upside down, the steel sheet should be clamped on and welded in place. Next, turn the chassis back the right way up and continue welding the sheet to the tubes on the inside transmission tunnel, on B1, B2 and C.

Steel sheet now needs to be cut for the sides of the transmission

Fig. 4.36. Nearside rear suspension brackets in place. Note the chassis mounting bracket for the Panhard rod, the rear suspension side panels and the fuel tank support strips already in place.

Fig. 4.37. Weld on strengthening fillets on the insides of the upper rear shock absorber mounts as above.

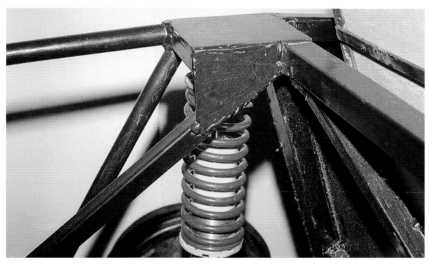

Fig. 4.38. Showing part of the steel flooring. Note centre seat belt mounting plates in position (a variation on Fig. 4.22). Note, also, brake pipe bracket in the top left quarter of the picture, and the cut out section at the back of the transmission tunnel to make room for the differential housing and universal joint.

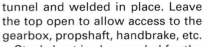

tunnel and welded in place. Leave the top open to allow access to the gearbox, propshaft, handbrake, etc.

Steel sheet is also needed for the footwell/bulkhead panels, and the rear suspension side panels. You now have a complete chassis.

Fabricate from 1in (25mm) wide x ⅛in (3mm) thick steel strip the curved sections that form the profile for your rear mudguards. You will need to match the curve to that of your mudguards. Using offcuts of 16swg steel sheet make a flange for the inside of each curve. This is to secure the trim, and will need to be drilled at appropriate points.

Fig. 4.39. View of chassis bottom with steel sheet in place.

Fig. 4.40. Panelled in curved rear wing support from the outside.

Fig. 4.41. Curved rear wing support from the inside.

Rust-inhibiting paint

The chassis should now be given a coat of rust-inhibiting paint. But first, use a sander to clean up any welding splatter, sharp edges or corners, and also sand down untidy welds. Great care must be taken when sanding welds not to remove so much metal that it weakens the weld. (If in doubt, seek expert advice.) The idea is to leave a flat smooth surface so that the aluminium panels will fit flush against the tubes, as any bumps or raised welds will distort and show as blemishes on the panels.

Building your chassis probably represents 50 per cent of the whole project. It is certainly the most labour intensive part of the construction of your car, as most other parts are now just bolted on.

Fig. 4.42. The chassis with a coat of rust-inhibiting paint. The curved rear wing supports had not been fitted to this chassis.

Fig. 4.43. Step by step.

CHAPTER 5

Steering

When you submit your car for its SVA test the inspector will look at your steering to make sure that it is designed in a way that prevents the column from causing you injury in the event of a head-on collision. This means that you must build in some form of energy absorption – either a collapsible or crushable column, a telescopic shaft, sliding clamps or an offset shaft. You will need at least two universal joints for an offset shaft. Your steering wheel must also be capable of absorbing energy on impact and, sadly (but in the interests of safety), fancy wheels with thin or perforated spokes will not be passed by the inspector. The argument is that whatever you are wearing might just get caught up in such steering wheels. The current *SVA Inspection Manual* sets out the criteria in detail.

Steering column and shaft

If you are fitting a Ford 1100, 1300 or 1600 engine, you can make use of the Escort donor car column, or one from a Vauxhall Nova or a Ford Sierra. It needs to be the sort which includes a steering lock, and it is also handy to fit a column which incorporates the switchgear and wiring for indicators, lights, windscreen washer/wiper and horn. Modifications will be necessary, of course, to suit your engine layout and to comply with regulations.

Unless your welding is up to a high standard I recommend that any modifications to the steering involving welding be carried out (or be carefully checked) by a qualified welder or engineer.

The necessary modification to the extension shaft calls for the existing shaft (with universal joints at each end) to be cut in half. The two ends are then welded on to a length of steel tube with ⅛in wall thickness. It is this operation which requires accuracy and expert welding.

The actual length of the tube will have to be determined by taking careful measurements once you are at rolling chassis stage with the steering rack fitted (see Chapter 13). The way to do this is to connect one half of the cut-in-half shaft (by way of the universal joint) to the steering column shaft, and the other half to the steering rack (the splines of the Nova or Sierra universal joints fit those on the Escort rack). Now measure the straight line between the cut ends of the two halves and add two inches to allow for a one-inch insertion at each end into the extension tube. This will give you the needed length of the extension tube.

Fig. 5.1. A Vauxhall Nova collapsible steering column with ignition switch steering lock and mounting for switchgear. The existing mounting bracket can be used to fit the column to your car. (Photo. Steve Williams)

Fig. 5.2. An Escort steering rack with a Sierra crushable column and collapsible shaft, a steel tube for extension purposes and top and bottom universal joint couplings. (Photo. Steve Williams)

Fig. 5.3. A Sierra column in situ showing crushable section. (Photo. Steve Williams)

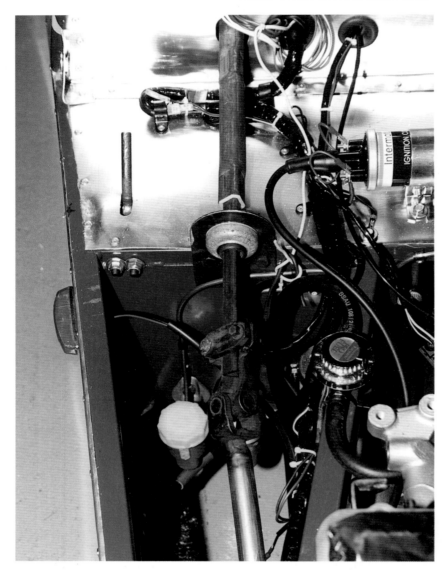

Fig. 5.4. A universal joint and sliding clamp linking an extension shaft to a steering column. (Photo. Steve Williams)

Fig. 5.5. A universal joint at the steering rack end of the extension shaft. (Photo. Steve Williams)

Steering rack

As mentioned in Chapter 3, before attaching the donor Escort steering rack to your chassis, fit new rubbers in the two steering rack mounting clamps, and replace the rubber ball-joint covers if they are damaged or perished. If the rubber bellows on the rack are damaged or leaky, replace them as well – it is not an expensive job.

CHAPTER 6

Modifying the rear axle and propshaft

You will be using the rear axle from your donor Mk I or Mk II Escort, and the first step is to strip it down, removing the brake assemblies, drive shafts and differential. The reason for this is not so much for overhaul, but to remove components that may be damaged when welding. Also, the two spring mounting plates should be hacksawed off, removing any remaining metal with a file or angle grinder (not forgetting to wear your clear goggles). Great care must be taken to ensure that you do not cut or grind into the surface of the axle casing as this could cause oil leaks or, in extreme cases, weaken the axle.

You now require two lengths of 2in x 2in (51mm x 51mm) RHS steel with a wall thickness of ⅛in (3mm). These will form the mountings for the four trailing arms and the Panhard rod which are part of the rear suspension system. Following the plan, drill two ⁷⁄₁₆in (11mm) diameter holes and cut a semi-circle corresponding to the curvature of the axle tube in each piece of RHS, and remove the front edge. Ensure that it fits snugly around the axle prior to welding.

I have found that the easiest way to cut out the semi-circle is to remove a triangle of metal with two hacksaw cuts and then file or angle grind away the remaining material. Alternatively, the brackets can be fabricated from steel strip cut,

drilled and welded together (*see Fig. 6.1*).

To reduce sideways movement of the axle, make the Panhard rod as long as possible.

Referring to the plans, the position of the new mountings must now be accurately marked on to the axle. Make sure that the axle is the right way up. This is not as silly as it may seem because, with all the brackets removed, the only way that you can tell is by the drain plug (which should be at the bottom) and the breather vent (which should be at the top). Find the centre of the axle casing by measuring the overall width and

halving the measurement. A scribed mark or dot punch will suffice. You must now accurately measure the distance between the trailing arm brackets on the chassis and position your new brackets on the axle. Measurement X must exactly equal measurement Y (see *Fig. 6.4*). Also ensure that they are parallel with the forward face of the axle casing.

Having positioned your brackets, I suggest you lightly tack weld them on and then recheck all your measurements to ensure they are correct before fully welding.

Now take your two remaining suspension mounting brackets,

Fig. 6.1. Two fabricated mounting brackets designed to fit the standard Ford Escort back axle. (Photo. Steve Williams)

71

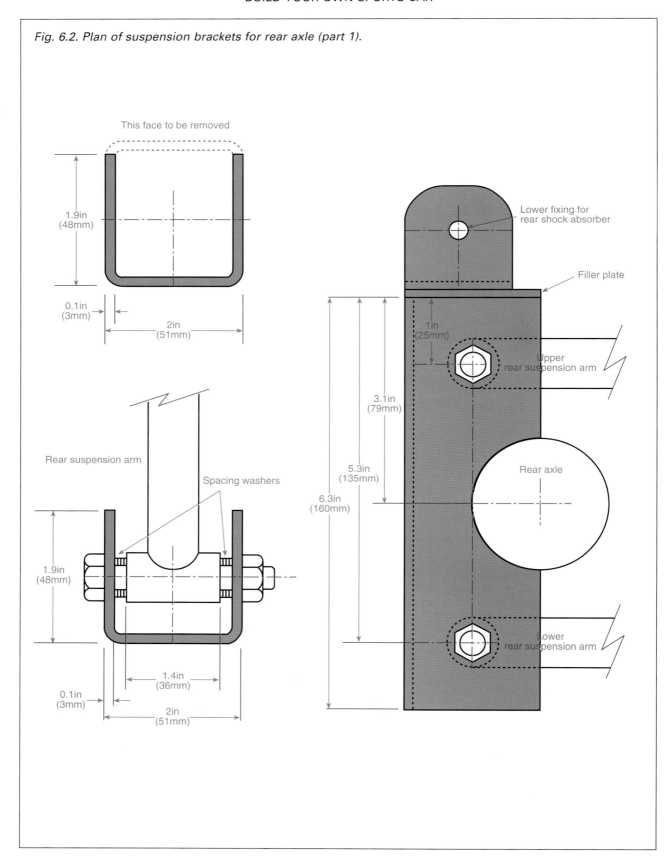

Fig. 6.2. Plan of suspension brackets for rear axle (part 1).

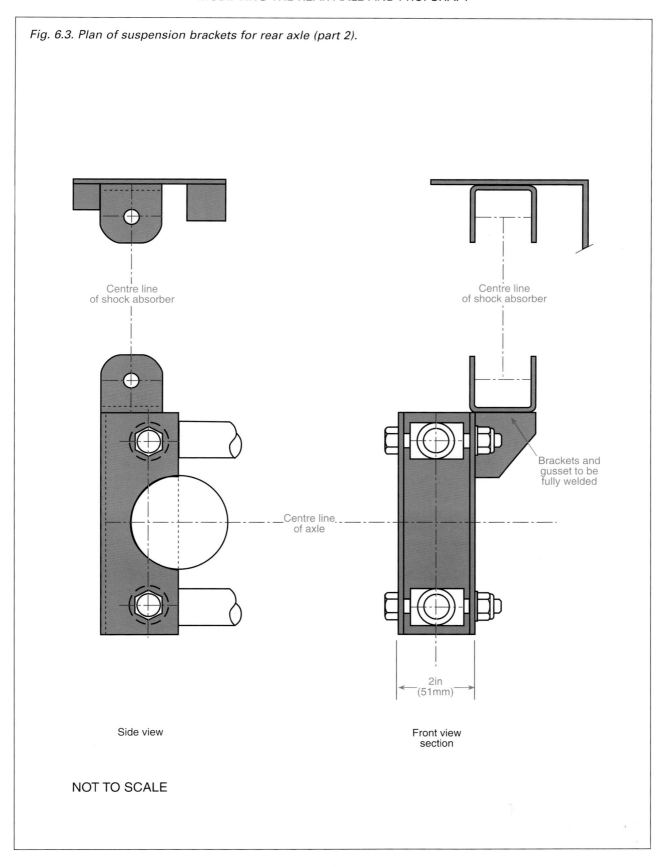

Fig. 6.3. Plan of suspension brackets for rear axle (part 2).

Centre line
of shock absorber

Centre line
of shock absorber

Brackets and
gusset to be
fully welded

Centre line
of axle

2in
(51mm)

Side view

Front view
section

NOT TO SCALE

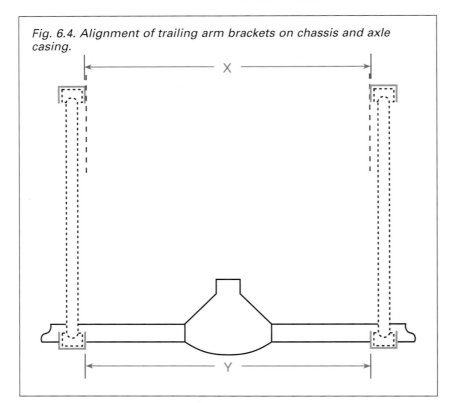

Fig. 6.4. Alignment of trailing arm brackets on chassis and axle casing.

position them and weld in place with ⅛in (3mm) thick strengthening fillets. See *Figs. 6.5 and 6.6* for how finished job should look.

Your modified axle is now complete and ready for reassembly. First, wash out the casing inside and out with a degreaser, and be sure you remove all traces of metal dust or swarf. Now is the time to check the serviceability of the wheel bearings, and also the wheel cylinders and brake linings, renewing as necessary. The final finish of the reassembled axle is your choice, but certainly some form of paint protection is needed.

Fig. 6.5. A nearside rear view of an axle modification. This shows a different mounting bracket arrangement from the one described. It had to be modified to make room for a longer shock absorber.

Fig. 6.6. An offside rear view of an axle modification with Panhard rod mounting welded into place and Panhard rod fitted, showing the different mounting bracket arrangement.

Fig. 6.7. A view from the front of an axle modification, using a variation on the mounting bracket described.

PROPSHAFT

Your propshaft is also sourced from the donor Escort, but it needs to be the single section type as used in the 1100 model, and you will have to shorten it. The two section version on the 1300 and 1600 models cannot be used, although the front and rear universal joints can be removed and fitted to a new piece of 16swg steel tube, or another old propshaft.

The propshaft transmits the drive from the gearbox to the back axle. As the axle moves up and down it travels through an arc, which means the propshaft has to 'lengthen' and 'shorten'. This is achieved by means of a sliding splined joint on the front of the propshaft which slides over a mating splined shaft on the rear of the gearbox, and to allow for the constant changing angles between gearbox and axle there is a universal joint at each end. So, any DIY modifications to the propshaft must be done with great care and absolute accuracy. It is in your own interest to get your work checked over by an expert. Alternatively, have the needed modifications carried out by a specialist.

If you are going to tackle the job yourself, you can do it with the tools used for building the chassis, but it will help to have access to an engineer's lathe for cutting the tube to the correct length and at a perfect right angle.

First make a note of the position of the universal joints. You will see that the yokes front and rear are in the same position on the tube in relation to each other. It is critical that the yokes are reassembled on the new tube in the same position.

With a hacksaw and files or (with extreme care and wearing goggles) an angle grinder, cut the front splined shaft, complete with universal joint and yoke casting, from the tube. This is best achieved by grinding or filing down the weld joining the yoke and tube together. The tube wall thickness is only about 16swg, so you do not have to go too far. About 1½in (38mm) back along the tube, cut through with a hacksaw. If you look down the tube towards the yoke, you will be able to see the amount of remaining tube which has to be removed. Now it is down to that patience I was telling you about, and careful use of file, hacksaw and grinder.

With the engine and axle fitted in the chassis, and the vehicle as near to its finished weight as possible (so that the axle is assuming its correct position) slide the splined shaft together with universal joint and yoke assembly as far as it will go over the mating spline on the rear of the gearbox. Then, from a fixed point, measure how far you have to pull it back before the splines clear each other. The measurement may vary slightly from gearbox to gearbox, but it will probably be about 4in (102mm). Subtract ½in (13mm) from this and divide by 2 – this makes 1¾in (44mm). The reason for subtracting ½in (13mm) is to prevent the propshaft from going 'solid' on the gearbox at maximum compression.

Now replace the splined shaft back into the gearbox and push it in 1¾in (44mm), and measure the distance to the rear axle driveshaft flange from where the tube was originally welded to the yoke, and this is the length the tube has to be cut to make up the modified propshaft.

As mentioned above, the tube is best cut, or parted off, on a lathe to ensure accuracy, but it can be done with careful marking and cutting by hand with a hacksaw.

Replace the yoke back in the tube. It should be a good fit and may need a little help from a soft hammer. Make sure that both yokes are aligned as in their original positions, then weld. It may help to first fix in position with four small tack welds around the tube, recheck for alignment and, if OK, then fully weld.

Although I have used this method many times on specials and racing cars with no ill effects or problems, I suggest it would be a good idea to have your handiwork checked by an expert and, if necessary, have it balanced.

Fig. 6.8. A propshaft fitted. This one was made from a split Ford Escort propshaft, with the front and rear joints removed and rewelded on to a suitable 16swg steel tube.

CHAPTER 7

Making the front and rear suspension units

The front suspension consists of double tubular wishbones and coil-over telescopic shock absorbers – by means of which the Ford Cortina hubs are attached to the space-frame chassis – and the rear suspension is a five link system comprising four trailing arms and a Panhard rod, also using coil-over shock absorbers, by which the Ford Escort rear axle is connected to the chassis.

The shock absorbers in our project car were the most difficult to source at a budget price, and the car was almost finished before I found a set from a trader at a kit car show. They were new but old stock. Of course, it seemed that as soon as I found them I promptly came across several other bargain sets.

All of the suspension components need to move freely, and are therefore fitted with some form of bearing surface at each moving point. The budget method uses metalastic bushes of the type shown on the right in *Fig. 7.2.*

These bushes fit into the bush

Fig. 7.1. A pair of shock absorbers which are adjustable for damper rate and ride height. They should have an extended length of 14in (356mm) minimum between bolt holes, and a compressed length of 10in (254mm) maximum between bolt holes. Coil springs should be rated at between 200lb and 220lb front and 180lb and 200lb rear. (Photo. Steve Williams)

Fig. 7.2. Two types of metalastic bush. The one on the right is a Triumph Herald type as used on the basic road car in this book. The bush on the left has an outer steel sleeve, and to use this type you will need larger diameter tubes at the end of your suspension arms. (Photo. Steve Williams)

Fig. 7.3. A 'male' spherical bearing with locknut. The bearing screws into a threaded hole and is fully adjustable. The 'female' type screws on to a threaded rod and is also adjustable. (Photo. Steve Williams)

plan to use your car in competitions such as sprints and hill climbs. Also there is a more positive feel, there being none of the sponginess associated with the use of rubber bushes. However, for normal road use the ride can be a little harsh.

If you do decide to use spherical bearings, the building jigs and general design will have to be modified from the instructions given below. Generally, I believe that it is unnecessary for a road car to use anything other than metalastic bushes as they isolate vibration and absorb torsional stress so well. However, by way of experiment, I made all the rear suspension on my son's car Rose jointed. It certainly made the car more positive, but the price paid was a harsher ride, more noise and vibration and considerably greater financial outlay.

Shock absorbers can be obtained with either metalastic bushes or spherical bearings.

tubes at the end of the suspension arms. Each bush needs to be an extremely tight fit into its bush tube (known as an interference fit).

An alternative to metalastic bushes (though not a budget one) is to use spherical bearings – often referred to as Rose joints, although Rose is the name of only one manufacturer. The advantage of spherical bearings is their adjustability which enables the suspension geometry (castor angles, camber angles and so on) to be quickly and easily altered. This is particularly useful if you

Fig. 7.4. Metalastic bushes on rear shock absorbers. (Photo. Steve Williams)

WHAT YOU NEED

- 3ft (1m) of seamless steel tube with 1in (25mm) outside diameter (o.d.) and $^{13}/_{16}$in (21mm) inside diameter (i.d.)

- 8ft (2.5m) of $^3/_4$in (19mm) x 16swg seamless steel tube

- 9ft (2.75m) of 1in (25mm) x 16swg seamless steel tube

- 6in (152mm) of 1in (25mm) round stock bar

- 18 x 1$^7/_{16}$in (36mm) wide Triumph Herald metalastic bushes with $^{13}/_{16}$in (21mm) o.d. and $^3/_8$in (9mm) i.d. (These are readily available from after-market specialist suppliers.)

- Offcuts of $^1/_8$in (3mm) steel plate

- 4 x coil-over shock absorbers

- 2 x right-hand threaded track rod ends from a Ford Transit van to act as top swivel joints

- 2 x bottom swivels from a Cortina Mk III, IV or V

Fig. 7.5. Top and bottom swivels. The top swivel (right) is a track rod end from a Ford Transit van, and the bottom swivel is from a Cortina (as fitted to Mk III, IV and V). Ensure that you use a Castleton nut with split pin, or a Nylock nut, to secure the swivel.

CUTTING TO LENGTH

Cut the 1in (25mm) o.d. tube into 18 lengths of 1⁷⁄₁₆in (36mm). (These will form the bush tubes into which the metalastic bushes are pressed, so it is essential that they are cut at right angles. You can do this by hand with a hacksaw, but the best method is to have them turned off on an engineer's lathe to ensure perfection.)

Cut four 13³⁄₈in (340mm) lengths of ³⁄₄in (19mm) x 16swg tube (bottom wishbone arms).

Cut two 7¼in (184mm) and two 7½in (191mm) lengths of ³⁄₄in (19mm) x 16swg tube (top wishbone arms).

Cut four 12in (305mm) lengths of 1in (25mm) x 16swg tube (rear suspension arms).

Cut a length of 38½in (978mm) of 1in (25mm) x 16swg tube (Panhard rod).

Cut two 1⁵⁄₈in (43mm) lengths of 1in (25mm) round stock bar. To cut the thread yourself you will need to machine out and tap a thread. A tap and handle can be hired from a tool hire shop. Alternatively get your bushes threaded for you by a local engineering company. (The thread needs to match the thread of the Ford Transit top swivels – M18 x 1.5 fine.)

From ⅛in (3mm) steel plate, cut out two spacer plates and two swivel joint plates (bottom wishbone). (See *Figs. 7.11* and *7.13* for shape and dimensions.)

Fig. 7.6. A ball joint from an Austin Maxi which can also be used as the bottom swivel on your Locost. The advantage is that it is lighter. (Photo. Steve Williams)

Fig. 7.7. Exploded view of front suspension assembly.

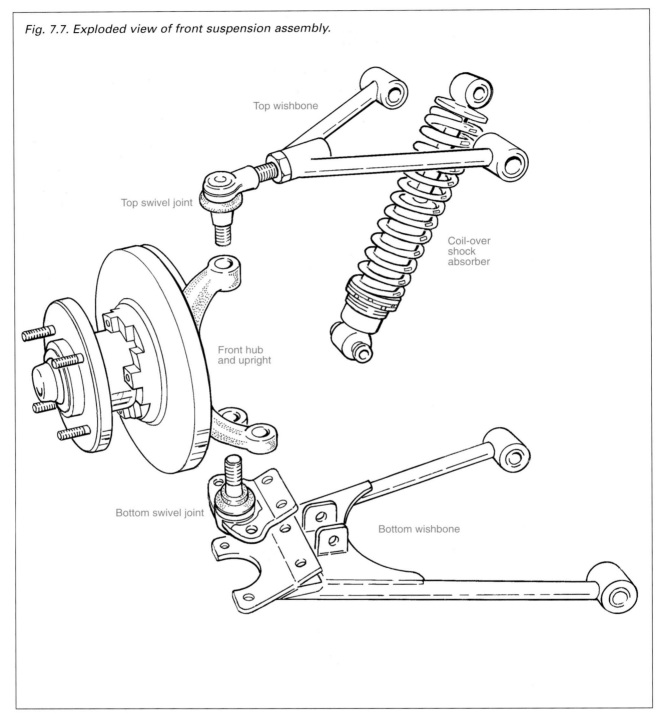

Top wishbone

Top swivel joint

Coil-over
shock
absorber

Front hub
and upright

Bottom swivel joint

Bottom wishbone

FRONT SUSPENSION

Bottom wishbone

Using a vice and following the plan, flatten one end of each of the four 13⅜in (340mm) lengths of ¾in (19mm) x 16swg steel tube.

The other ends of the four wishbone tubes must be profiled with a round file, as shown, to make a good fit to the bush tubes.

To get the angles right you need to make a jig from either ¼in (6mm) steel plate and ⅛in (3mm) angle iron, or from blockboard and 1½in x 1in x 1in (38mm x 25mm x 25mm) wooden blocks (see Fig. 7.9. Whether you use steel or wood, the base must be 18in (457mm) square. Weld the angle iron to the plate in positions ABC and DEF, or if wood is used, screw and glue the blocks in the same positions. Drill ⅜in (9mm) holes at locations G and H and weld or glue ⅛in (3mm) thick spacer strips to support the arms at the correct

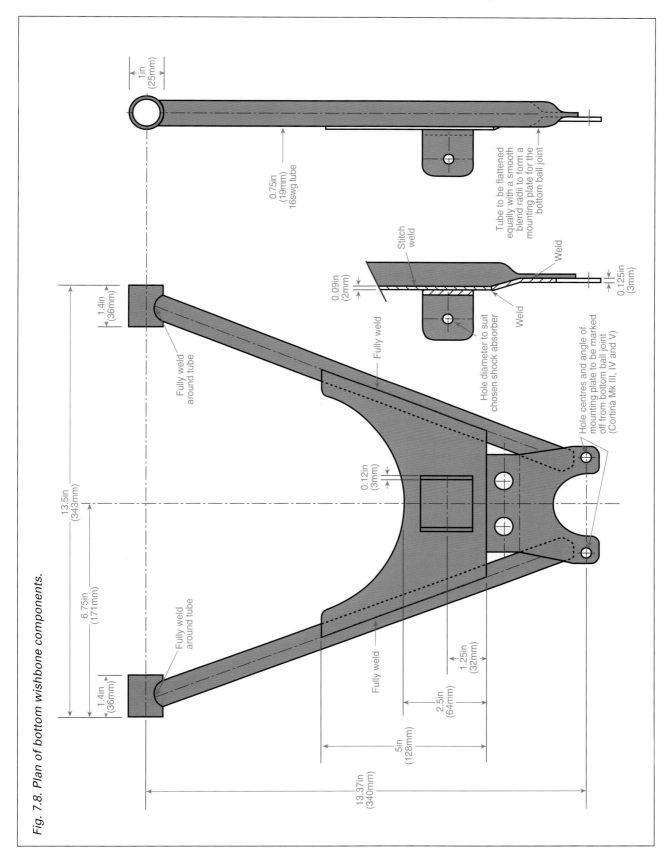

Fig. 7.8. Plan of bottom wishbone components.

1in (25mm)

0.75in (19mm) 16swg tube

Tube to be flattened equally with a smooth blend radii to form a mounting plate for the bottom ball joint

Stitch weld

0.09in (2mm)

Weld

Fully weld

Weld

0.125in (3mm)

Hole diameter to suit chosen shock absorber

Hole centres and angle of mounting plate to be marked off from bottom ball joint (Cortina Mk III, IV and V)

1.4in (36mm)

Fully weld around tube

13.5in (343mm)

6.75in (171mm)

0.12in (3mm)

Fully weld around tube

Fully weld

1.4in (36mm)

1.25in (32mm)

2.5in (64mm)

5in (128mm)

13.37in (340mm)

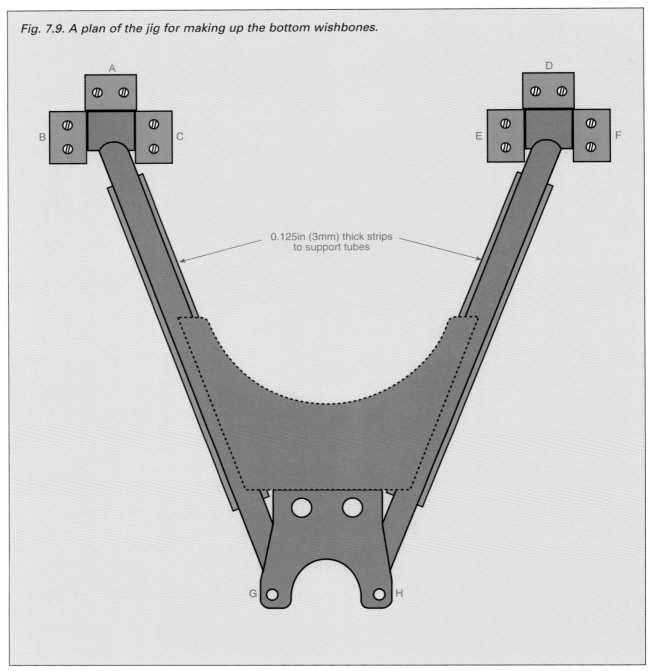

Fig. 7.9. A plan of the jig for making up the bottom wishbones.

0.125in (3mm) thick strips to support tubes

height. This will bring the main wishbone tubes to the centre of the bush tubes.

Having made your jig, place two bush tubes in position and locate the swivel joint plate over the holes in the jig and drop two ⅜in (9mm) bolts through the corresponding holes, but do not fit nuts or tighten by any other means.

Next, position left and right 13⅜in (340mm) wishbone tubes in the jig, ensuring that they form a tight fit to the bush tubes, and with flattened ends under the swivel joint plate.

You can now tack weld the main wishbone tubes to the bush tubes (one tack each).

Next, place the steel spacer plate in position on top of the wishbone tubes and touching the swivel joint plate, and tack weld the four components together.

At this stage you need to check that all components are correctly aligned. If so, the assembly can be removed from the jig. Turn it over and tack weld the other side. Replace it in the jig, check again, and if still satisfactory fully weld all the joints.

Finally weld in the shock absorber mounting.

Repeat the process for the second bottom wishbone.

Top wishbone

Construct a second jig for the top wishbone (see *Fig. 7.12*).

Shape the ends of the tubes as shown in the plan, and fit bush tubes, wishbone tubes and threaded bush on to the jig. Check alignment and, if good, weld the components together. Take care not to damage the internal thread of the threaded bush.

Repeat the process for the second top wishbone.

The top ball joints (ex-Ford Transit track rod ends), screwed

Fig. 7.10. A carbon steel tap for cutting the thread in the top wishbone bush into which the top swivel screws. (Photo. Steve Williams)

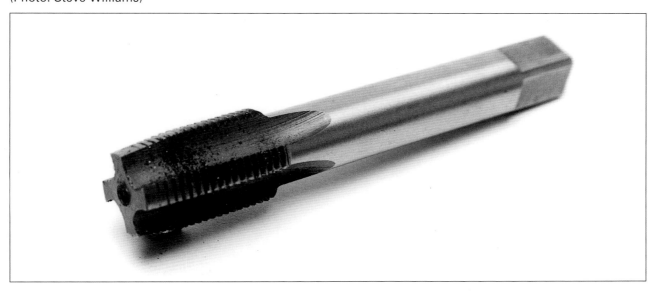

Fig. 7.11. Plan of top wishbone components. Note the greater angle of the right arm from the centre line. This is the built-in castor angle (see also Fig. 13.7).

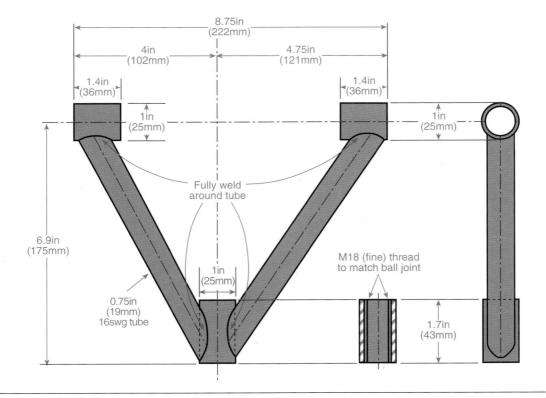

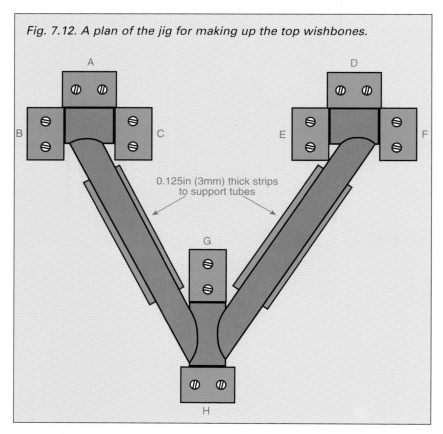

Fig. 7.12. A plan of the jig for making up the top wishbones.

A

D

B

C

E

F

0.125in (3mm) thick strips
to support tubes

G

H

into the top wishbones and secured with locking nuts, permit adjustment of the camber angle. The optimum measurement is zero, but you could have up to 3° neg, which may improve cornering but will probably decrease tyre life. The toe-in should be set at 1° with an acceptable variation of ±0.1°. If your chassis and wishbones have been built accurately, the castor angle should be 5.30°, but a variation of ±0.3° is acceptable.

Fig. 7.13. Offside front suspension in situ. The top mounting for the coil-over shock absorber has been changed to accommodate a longer unit.

Fig. 7.14. Nearside front suspension in situ. The top mounting for the coil-over shock absorber has been changed to accommodate a longer unit.

Fig. 7.15. To be on the safe side, any potential harm that an SVA test inspector might see in bolt ends at the front of the car can be removed by attaching domed plastic bolt-covers. (Photo. Steve Williams)

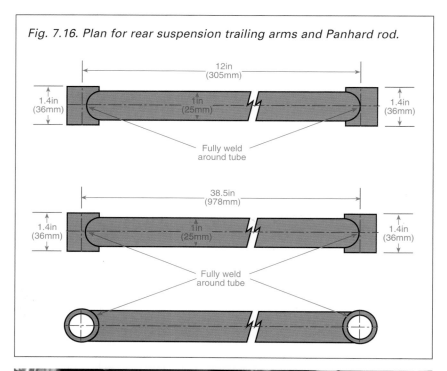

Fig. 7.16. Plan for rear suspension trailing arms and Panhard rod.

REAR SUSPENSION

No jig is necessary to make the five rear suspension components, but great care must be taken to ensure that all four trailing arms are of identical length (12in/305mm), otherwise the rear wheels will be out of alignment. Profile the ends of the rods to take the bush tubes, and tack weld a bush tube to one end only of each arm. You can then check equality of length by pushing a dowel rod horizontally through the bush tubes, allowing the arms to hang. All arms being equal, weld on the bush tubes to the remaining ends.

The Panhard rod is made in the same way but is best left until the rear axle has been fitted to the chassis with the four trailing arms, shock absorbers and road wheels. When this stage has been reached, adjust the chassis so that the distance is equal on both sides between rear wheel rims and the chassis, and measure between Panhard rod mounting holes on chassis and axle. This distance is the length required for your Panhard rod between bush centres (see also Chapter 6 on the rear axle). As a rough guide, it will be around 38½in (978mm).

You will now have to decide on the finish for your suspension components – two coats of primer and two coats of gloss. In such an exposed position on the car, some type of protection is essential.

Once painted you can press the 18 metalastic bushes into the bush tubes. A vice and two sockets work quite well for this job, though you will need a second pair of hands.

Fig. 7.17. Rear suspension. When the car is built up and at its full weight the trailing links should be horizontal.

CHAPTER 8

Adapting the exhaust system

Two types of exhaust system were fitted to the Mk I and Mk II Escorts – one with a silencer only and one with a silencer and expansion box. In both cases the standard exhaust manifold can be used, but you will not need the expansion box. The front pipe must be shortened and turned below the manifold to allow it to exit through the nearside lower side panel. The remainder of the system can be cut and welded to fit, ensuring that the silencer is as far from the manifold as possible.

Assemble the exhaust pipe at open-chassis stage and plot the position for cutting a 2½in (64mm) hole in the body panel (see Chapter 12).

The silencer should be attached to the chassis with made-up mounting brackets incorporating a metalastic rubber exhaust mounting (see *Fig. 8.4*) called a cotton reel (the type normally fitted to the tail pipe of the Mini). A short tail pipe should be made, exiting in front of the nearside rear wing at an angle to deflect gases to the side (see *Fig. 8.3*).

A heat shield must be fitted to protect both passengers and pedestrians from the hot silencer. This can be made from a piece of 18swg steel or aluminium sheet, suitably curved and fixed to the silencer using two jubilee clips. You will need to spot weld three flanges on the inside of the shield for each

Fig. 8.1. Shows a standard Escort 1100 or 1300 exhaust manifold and modified front section of exhaust pipe.

jubilee clip to pass through (see *Fig. 8.5*). Allow a ½in (13mm) air gap between the silencer and the shield.

It may be that your donor vehicle's exhaust system is past its best. If this is the case, you can make your own system. Straight lengths of exhaust pipe can be purchased, together with a silencer, from most motor factors. When completed, and after satisfying yourself it is a good fit, wire brush the whole system and spray with

Fig. 8.2. A four-branch manifold and front section of exhaust pipe from a 1300GT Escort.

Fig. 8.5. Cross section of silencer with heat shield secured by a jubilee clip passing through three made up flanges spot welded to the inside of the shield.

Flange
(spot welded to inside of heat shield)

0.5in
(13mm)

Heat shield

0.5 in
(13mm)

Jubilee clip

Silencer

Fig. 8.3. An exhaust tail pipe bend. Note the rear bracket on the silencer attached to the chassis bracket using a 'cotton reel' bush.

Fig. 8.4. A cotton reel metalastic exhaust mounting (normally fitted to support a Mini tail pipe).

heat resistant paint (available in aerosol cans from car accessory shops).

When you take your car for its SVA test your exhaust system will be subject to the inspector's scrutiny by way of both a visual check and the use of a gas analyser to measure exhaust emissions. To find out exactly what is required of your particular car, refer to the current edition of the *SVA Inspection Manual*.

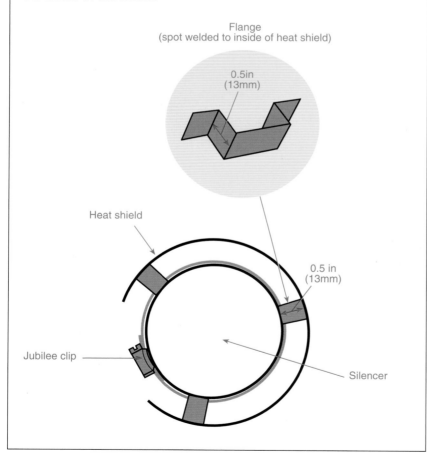

Fig. 8.6. A heat shield made from the stainless steel drum of an old washing machine. (Photo. Steve Williams)

Fig. 8.7. An SVA-compliant heat shield which can be bought ready-made. (Photo. Steve Williams)

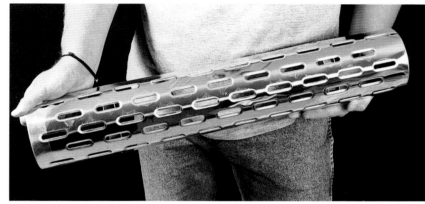

Fig. 8.8. A four-two-one exhaust manifold with connecting pipe suitably adapted.

CHAPTER 9

Modifications to the cooling system

For the most part the components for your cooling system will be sourced by the Ford Escort Mk I or Mk II donor car, but unless they are in very good condition it is worth renewing connecting hoses and clips.

WHAT YOU NEED
- Radiator
- Connecting hoses
- Jubilee clips
- Electric fan
- $\frac{5}{16}$in x 1in (8mm x 25mm) bolts
- Nylock nuts
- Washers
- Ford Fiesta thermostat housing
- Black paint (matt finish)

RADIATOR
First, check that your radiator is in good condition, with no visible signs of damage or leaks.

Hold it up to a bright light and look directly through the gills. Quite often these become blocked with a mixture of oil, dirt and dust, which restricts the airflow through the radiator and hence its cooling efficiency. If it is blocked, soak the radiator in a bath of paraffin, or one of the proprietary engine degreasers, and then gently hose it through. This usually clears it.

You will probably want to repaint

Fig. 9.1. The donor car radiator trial-fitted to the chassis, showing the position of the top and bottom mounting brackets.

your radiator, and the best colour to use is matt black as this permits heat to dissipate more readily.

Once all this is done, you can fix the radiator to the mounting brackets on the chassis frame with the ⁵⁄₁₆in x 1in (8mm x 25mm) bolts, washers and Nylock nuts.

If you are unable to find hoses long enough, lengths of steel, copper or aluminium tube with short rubber hose at each end can be used. Make sure the pipe is secured by cable ties or large 'P' clips, otherwise the top hose connection on the radiator might be broken off.

THERMOSTAT

Fit a Ford Fiesta thermostat (including the temperature sender unit) as shown in *Fig. 9.2* in place of the Escort version. This should bolt on without any modification.

ELECTRIC FAN

Fit the electric fan that you have had to acquire and connect up the temperature sender unit in the Fiesta thermostat via a Ford fan switch (Ford Part No. 6144361).

If you decide to use a rear-mounted fan, then suitable brackets will need to be welded to the chassis to hold it as close as possible to the radiator, taking care to avoid the steering rack. For a front-mounted fan use can be made of the existing radiator mounting bolts.

The first fan on my son's Locost was from a Lancia and was rear mounted. It worked well, but clearance between the fan and the steering rack was minimal. Later I chanced upon a new Bosch fan at a car boot sale for £2. It fitted superbly and was so powerful that we used to think that if ever we ran out of petrol it would quite likely propel us to the next filling station!

Fig. 9.2. A Ford Fiesta thermostat housing fitted to an Escort engine. On the Locost it is necessary to fill the cooling system through this by unscrewing the top, because the radiator itself is set at too low a level.

Fig. 9.3. Electric fan fitting – four strips of 1in x ⅛in steel strip welded to fan cowling, drilled and secured to chassis with radiator mounting bolts.

CHAPTER 10

Making the fuel tank

Materials required:

4ft x 4ft (1.25m x 1.25m) sheet steel or aluminium

5ft (1.5m) of 1in x ⅛in (25mm x 3mm) steel strip

5ft (1.5m) of 1in x ⅛in (25mm x 3mm) rubber strip

Fuel cap

Steel tube with bend diameter to suit filler cap

Rubber hose of a diameter to suit steel tube

4 hose clips to suit rubber hose

¼in x 2½in (6mm x 64mm) tube

Since the Escort fuel tank is the wrong shape, you will have to fabricate your own. However, I know of one Locost builder who successfully fitted a Mini van fuel tank into the space available, so it may be worth a visit to a few scrapyards to see what is available.

If you take the make-your-own route, the type of material you use will depend on your welding ability and the welding equipment. I imagine that most builders will opt for mild steel, although you can use aluminium. However, welding aluminium is difficult and requires great skill and some experience.

Cut your material according to the dimensions given in the plan (*Fig. 10.1*) and, for the main tank body, make four folds along the length as shown. Next, cut out and fold the end plates, taking care to fold the ½in (13mm) lips in opposite directions for each end.

Cut and fold the central baffle in the same way, but cut out the bottom corners to allow fuel to move from one side of the tank to the other. A piece of tube, 2in (51mm) or 3in (76mm) long, will be required for the filler neck. If this is unobtainable, a piece of flat sheet can be rolled into a cylinder of the required diameter and welded.

It is essential that the tank is welded to an exceptionally high standard to avoid leaks. If you are in any doubt about your own ability, then ask a professional welder to do it for you.

Welding sequence

1. Weld the long continuous seam along the top of the tank.
2. Secure in place the end furthest away from the fuel filler position, making sure all four edges are flush, and fully weld the edges.
3. Position the baffle at approximately the centre of the tank and tack weld into position. It is not essential to fully weld or to ensure a tight fit as the baffle doesn't have to be leak proof – it is there to prevent fuel surge from one end of the tank to the other.
4. Mark the position where the filler tube is to go, cut out the centre slightly smaller than the tube, place the tube in position and weld.
5. If a fuel gauge is required, you must obtain a 3in (76mm) disc of ³⁄₁₆in (5mm) thick metal on which to mount the sender unit. The centre must be cut out to allow the float to pass through, and holes must be drilled and tapped to suit the sender unit. Depending on whether your sender is top or side mounted, you can cut out a hole in the top of the tank or in the remaining end, position the sender mounting over the hole and weld.
6. Drill a hole in the front edge of the tank about ¼in (6mm) above base and fit in an outlet tube and weld in position. The ¼in (6mm) above base will ensure the pump does not pick up any sediment from the bottom of the tank.
7. Finally, weld on the remaining end.

The completed tank can be pressure tested with the aid of a bicycle pump attached to the outlet pipe, and with the sender unit fitted, and the filler neck bunged up, wet all the welded joints with soapy water. If you pump the tank up to 2 or 3psi, any leaks will be shown as bubbles, or alternatively there are proprietary crack-testing materials from specialist suppliers. These are essentially liquid dyes which you pour into the tank.

Important: Do not be tempted to pump the tank up with anything other than a bicycle hand or foot pump, and only using five or six strokes.

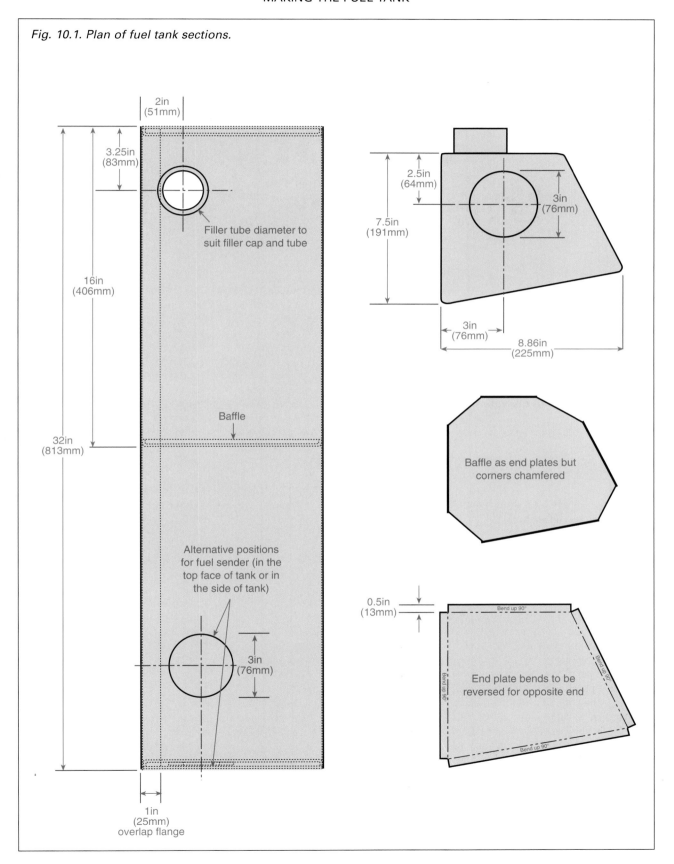

Fig. 10.1. Plan of fuel tank sections.

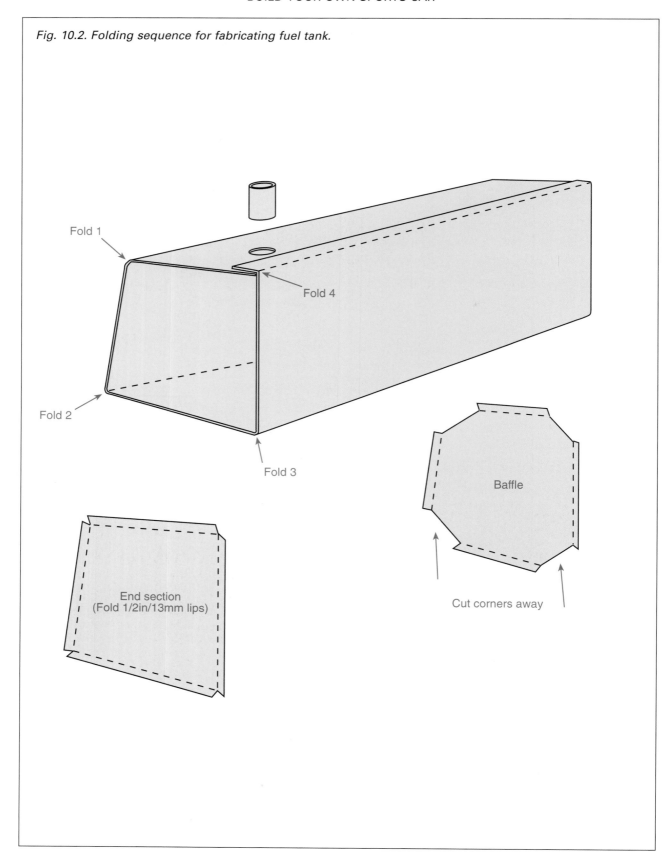

Fig. 10.2. Folding sequence for fabricating fuel tank.

Fig. 10.3. Test fitting the folded fuel tank prior to welding. Note, the car shown has independent rear suspension.

Fig. 10.4. The completed fuel tank. Note the filler neck, outlet pipe and sender unit. The $^{3}/_{16}$in (5mm) aluminium disc held in the right hand was welded in position to provide a mounting for the sender unit.

Fig. 10.5. Two completed fuel tanks. The smaller one is for race use. (Photo. Steve Williams)

CHAPTER 11

Making the nose cone and mudguards

Most of the body panels for the Locost are formed from aluminium using simple single curves. However, the nose cone and front and rear wings have compound curves (curved in more than one direction). To make these of metal would call for special presses or panel-beating skills and tools. The alternative is to mould such shapes in glassfibre.

Before progressing further, it is worth pointing out other options:

1. If funds allow, new items can be purchased. Many companies make kit cars not unlike our car, and would be pleased to sell you what you need. Most of them advertise in the kit car magazines. Also, with the ever growing number of Locosters there are now companies who manufacture parts, including nose cones and mudguards, specifically for the Locost.

2. Sometimes new or shop-soiled nose cones and mudguards are offered for sale at autojumbles, and damaged ones are frequently offered which can be easily repaired and repainted.

3. Trailer wings of the correct size are readily available from trailer suppliers in a range of materials, such as vacuum formed plastic, glassfibre, steel and aluminium. These look good and are easy to fit.

What you will need
Glassfibre materials are quite inexpensive if purchased in bulk direct from the suppliers. Don't be tempted to buy the packaged 'Repair Kits' on sale in car accessory shops, as you will need lots of them and the cost will be greatly increased. However, they are ideal if you only want a small quantity for repair work.

Materials:
Chopped strand matting
Hardener

Resin
Cellulose thinners (for cleaning brushes, etc.)
Release wax
Dzus fasteners

Tools:
Plastic or polythene container (a washing-up bowl will do)
Scissors
Mixing sticks (ice lolly sticks will do)
Cheap paint brushes

Fig. 11.1. Side view of nose cone showing cut-outs for headlamp bar and wishbones. Note also the hole drilled in the bottom left-hand corner on to which a Dzus can be riveted.

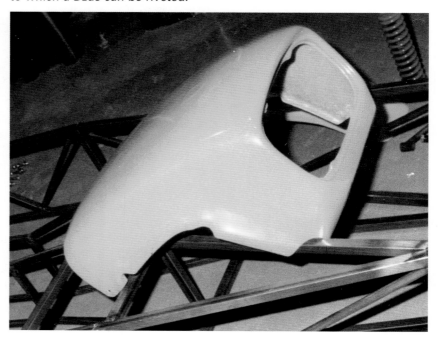

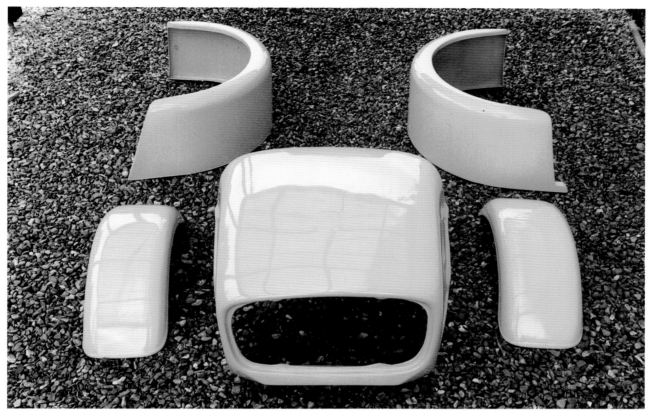

This is a messy job, so protective clothing and plenty of newspaper will be needed.

First we must have a mould or former from which to take our shape. For the front and rear wings I have used trailer wings for this purpose, but for the nose cone I had to start from scratch and build the shape up on the car. This is called a 'buck' in car factories, and they are usually sculpted in clay. Mine was more of an experiment and made from polystyrene blocks stuck together with PVA glue, and stuck to the front of the chassis. This was carved to shape with a bread-knife and a hacksaw blade until I got it about right. The whole was then given a light coat of plaster of Paris, carefully sanded down to a smooth finish and then given several coats of primer/filler and left to dry for a week. It was then lightly rubbed down with very fine wet and dry automotive paint finishing paper, well wet with soapy water. Great care must be taken as the paint and plaster

Fig. 11.2. The finished glassfibre nose cone and mudguards ready for attachment. (Photo. Steve Williams)

Fig. 11.3. A Dzus fastener and spring clip. Use these, with suitably positioned brackets, to secure the nose cone to the chassis. (Photo. Steve Williams)

coating is only eggshell thin, and too much pressure could break or crack the surface.

When I was satisfied with the overall shape and finish, and the 'buck' was thoroughly dry, I applied a coat of release wax with a soft cloth, making sure that I did not

miss any area. The purpose of the wax is to ensure the glassfibre does not stick to the 'buck' – almost the same as a cook greasing the inside of a baking tin before pouring in the cake mix.

Mix up a quantity of resin and hardener, and paint over the 'buck',

Fig. 11.4. To be doubly sure of pleasing the inspector at the SVA test centre you could fit coloured plastic trim to the leading edge of your front mudguards. (Photo. Steve Williams)

covering the whole area. Now saturate your pre-cut pieces of strand matting and lay over the 'buck', being careful to obtain a uniform thickness of about two layers with no dry areas or trapped air bubbles, and ensuring that it extends over the edges of the 'buck'.

When the glassfibre has fully hardened, or cured (see manufacturer's instructions) you will be able to pull the glassfibre mould from the 'buck'. The overlapping edges will need to be cut back to the original shape with a hacksaw blade and finally sanded to a smooth edge.

You will notice the nice smooth finish is on the inside, and the outside is a little bumpy and rough. What we now have is a female mould. You now have a decision to make. A manufacturer or professional would now make a new mould by waxing the inside and laying up the resin and matting in exactly the same way as before. When removed, the new mould will have a good finish where you want it – on the outside. The advantage of this is that you now have a mould to make additional mouldings. But, if you prefer to work with the first mould, you can spread a light layer of car body filler over the rough outside and, when dry, sand it down to a smooth finish.

CHAPTER 12

Body panels

MATERIALS REQUIRED

Three 8ft x 4ft (2.5m x 1.25m) sheets of 18swg half hard aluminium or the equivalent of second-hand aluminium cut from scrap.

Large tube of silicone bath sealant.

About 500 ⅜in (9mm) long x ⅛in (3mm) diameter aluminium pop rivets.

10ft x ½in x ⅛in (3m x 13mm x 3mm) mild steel strip.

TOOLS REQUIRED

Drill (hand-operated or electric)

Two ⅛in (3mm) drill bits

A straight edge or 3ft (1m) rule

Tape measure

Soft hammer (plastic, nylon or hide)

G-clamps

Set square

Two 5ft (1.5m) lengths of 2in x 1in (50mm x 25mm) planed soft wood

One 2ft x 2in x 2in (610mm x 50mm x 50mm) piece of soft wood

One 13in x 2in x 2in (330mm x 50mm x 50mm) piece of soft wood.

In my opinion, making the body panels is the most pleasing and rewarding job of the whole project. Your space-frame chassis suddenly looks like a motor car instead of a framework of tubes. It is also clean and light work which means you can do the odd hour here and there without having to get changed into your old working clothes.

It takes one person about 15–20 hours to make and fit all the panels, although this does not include the time taken to make the louvres on the bonnet – more on that later.

There are two ways to tackle this job, both equally as good. One way does not require any bending or forming of the aluminium, but rows of rivet heads will show. The other way requires folding the aluminium around the tubes and riveting on the inside, which keeps the rivet heads hidden. It is a matter of choice which method you use.

SIDE PANELS

The first panels to tackle are the chassis sides. On the outside they are flat faced with just one bend (actually more of a crease). If you do not want rivets showing, make the panels 16in x 50in (406mm x 1.25m). The sides of the space-frame chassis are only 13in (330mm) high, but the extra 3in (76mm) gives a 1in (25mm) fold at the bottom and two 1in (25mm) folds over the top tubes (J1/J2 and N1/N2 on chassis plan). To fold the aluminium, mark with a pencil a line 1in (25mm) from the bottom and a line 2in (50mm) from the top. If you are using reclaimed aluminium, keep the best side to the outside. Take your two lengths of 2in x 1in (50mm x 25mm) soft wood and sandwich either side of the panel, then clamp tightly with G-clamps. Because the metal is fairly soft you can start bending it by hand. Once you have bent it as far as you can, take the 2ft x 2in x 2in (610mm x 50mm x 50mm) block of soft wood and lay it lengthwise along the partly folded edge and strike the wood with your soft hammer, working along the whole panel until it is turned over at 90 degrees. The process is repeated for the other edge but with 2in (50mm) protruding. (See Fig. 12.1)

The panel can now be offered up to the chassis with the 1in lip at the bottom and the 2in (50mm) lip at the top. Line up the panel flush with the rear edge of suspension support tube M, and mark the position of the rear wing curved support strip which will prevent the aluminium fitting over top tube N. A small portion of aluminium will need to be cut away with tin snips to allow the panel to fit around the curved strip (see Figure 12.2). The panel will now fit tight against tubes A and N. Hold firmly in place and mark the position of tube H – the panel will need bending at this point. At the marked position, make V-shape cut-outs in both the 1in (25mm) and 2in (50mm) lips to allow the panel to bend. Now clamp two pieces of 13in x 2in x 1in (330mm x 50mm x 25mm) soft wood either side of the panel along

99

Fig. 12.1. 1. Securing an aluminium sheet with two lengths of soft wood and G-clamps. 2. First press down by hand … 3. then hammer it over to a right-angle using the 2in (50mm) square soft wood block.

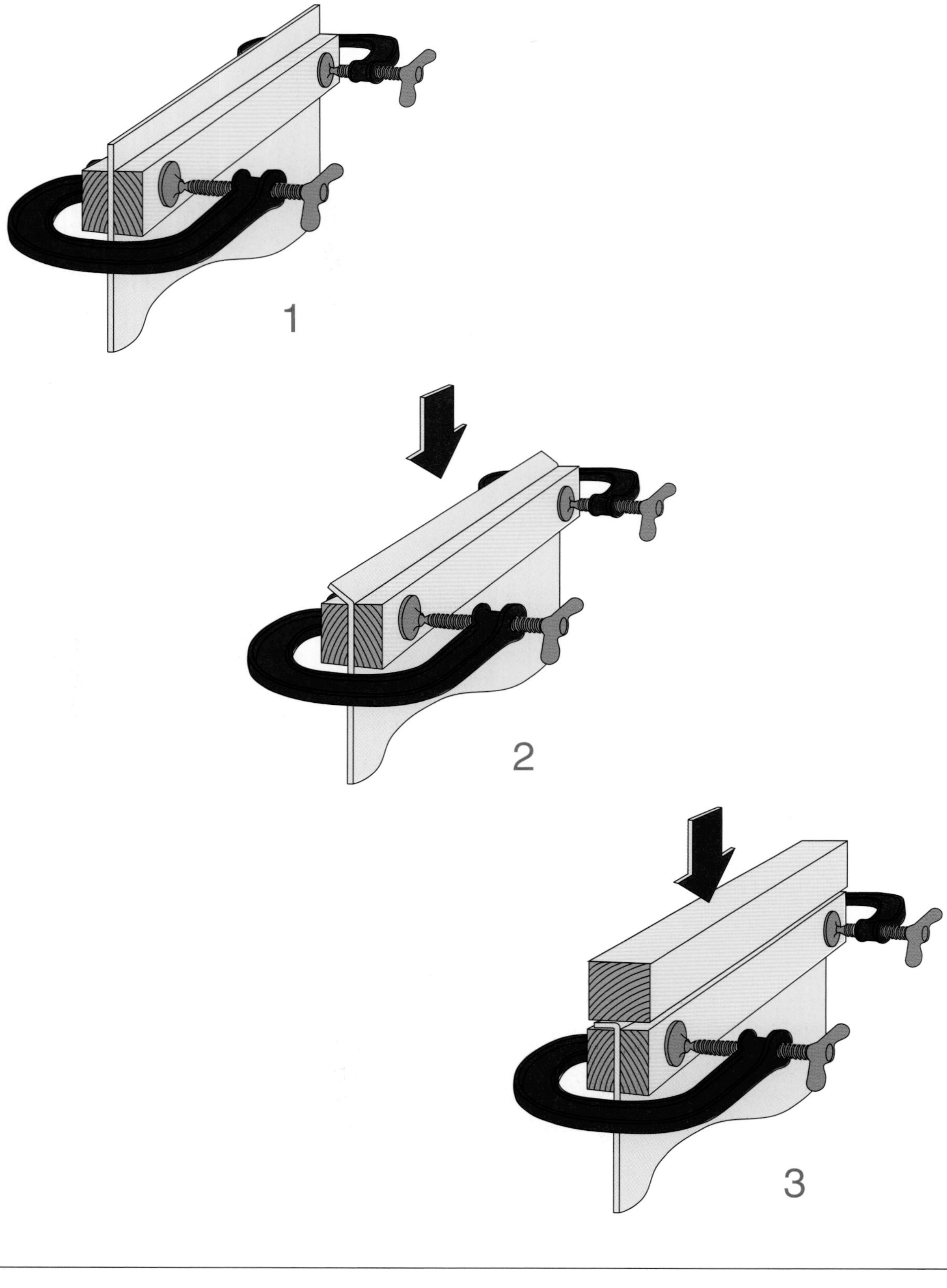

Fig. 12.2. Shows the cutaway needed to allow for the rear wing curved support strip.

the bend line and bend slightly by hand to an angle corresponding to the shape of the chassis. The panel should now fit snugly to the chassis. Secure in place by drilling and riveting to the top and bottom of upright tube M, and also underneath either side of the V cut-out at tube H.

Now, by hand, bend over to the inside the protruding 1in of panel lip on the top chassis rail and finally dress down with the 13in x 2in x 1in (330mm x 50mm x 25mm) soft wood and soft hammer. Now drill out the temporary securing rivets and remove the panel. Using silicone bath sealer (or similar) apply a bead of sealer to all interior panel edges, refit and locate the panel by re-riveting previously drilled holes. The purpose of the bath sealer is to damp down vibration noise, and it also acts as an adhesive. Finally, drill and rivet at 2in (50mm) intervals inside the upper 1in (25mm) lip and underfloor 1in (25mm) lip at the rear on suspension tube M. The panel can be riveted on the outside because this join is covered by the rear wing. (See *Figs. 12.3* to *12.5*)

Fig. 12.3. A full side panel riveted in place, showing the bend.

The easier method is to cut out a 13in x 50in (330mm x 1.25m) side panel, fold slightly at tube H, seal with silicone, and rivet directly to the outside of the chassis rails.

Fig. 12.4. A full side panel seen from the inside.

Fig. 12.5. A fitted side panel seen from underneath.

Fig. 12.6. Panelling around the transmission tunnel.

Fig. 12.7. A general view of side and behind seat panelling.

Fig. 12.8. Rear view of behind seat panelling.

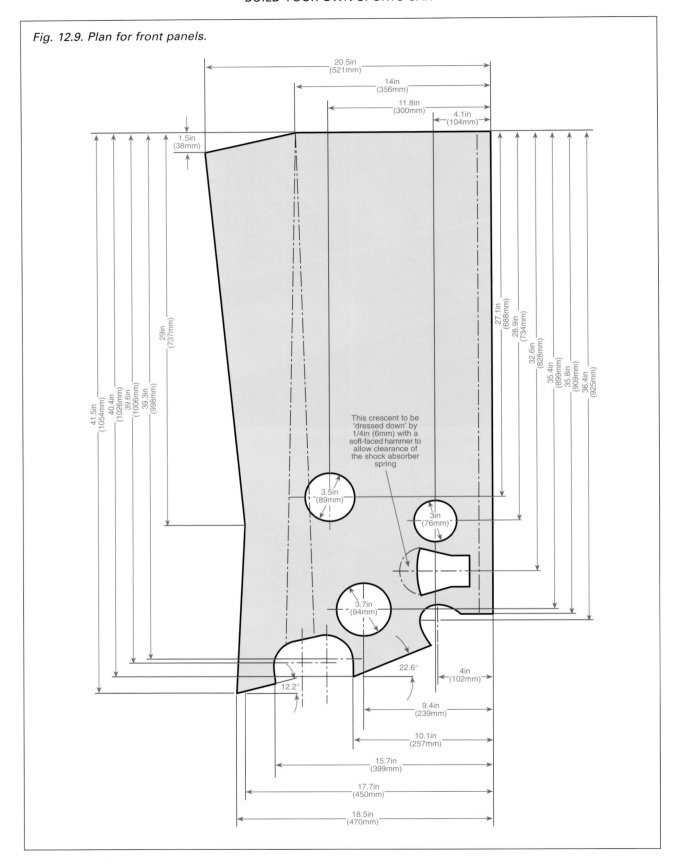

Fig. 12.9. Plan for front panels.

Fig. 12.10. A cardboard template was first made (foreground), the pattern then being transferred to sheet aluminium (centre) and finally riveted to the chassis (top).

FRONT PANELS

The front panels are complicated a little by the need to cut out holes for the wishbones, steering rack and shock absorbers (see *Fig. 12.10* for shape and position of holes). It is therefore best to make a pattern from thin card, tape this in position on the chassis and trial fit these components to ensure adequate clearance, particularly when you move the wishbones up and down. Once satisfactory clearances have been achieved, the card can be used as a pattern, and the shape transferred to aluminium sheet for cutting and fitting by either of the two methods described above (see *Fig. 12.9*). The bottom part of the aperture for the shock absorber top mounting needs to be 'dressed down' slightly with a soft-faced hammer. This is to allow clearance of the shock absorber spring. Only about ¼in (6mm) indentation is needed.

The side panels with the suspension cut-outs will overlap the cockpit side panels by 1in at forward tube H, and both panels will be riveted together into tube H.

To cut the hole for the exhaust pipe in the correct position in the nearside panel, measure from the exhaust ports on the cylinder head to the centre line of the pipe where it passes through, and make a 2½in (64mm) hole at the required depth and position where the pipe passes through. If necessary, enlarge the hole to be sure that the exhaust pipe does not touch the bodywork when the engine moves on its mountings under running conditions.

Fig. 12.11. An inside view of a fitted front panel with nose cone in situ. Note that the insides of the aluminium panels were not painted. This saves paint and the bare metal reflects more light into the engine bay. Note also the nose cone fixing brackets on the chassis top rails, and the Dzus fasteners.

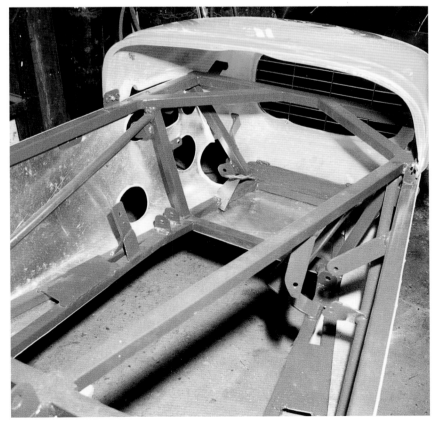

Fig. 12.12. The edges of the rear panel being dressed around the round tube with a soft-faced hammer. Ensure that the panel is supported in position, but take care if using clamps as they can easily mark the panel.

Fig. 12.13. A completed rear panel.

REAR PANEL

The rear panel has single curvatures where it wraps round the back. I recommend you first make a card pattern and, when satisfied with the fit, transfer the shape to your aluminium sheet. The bottom edge has a 1in (25mm) right-angle fold made by the method described above, and a series of V cuts will have to be made to allow it to follow the curves of the rear chassis members. The treatment of the top and ends of this panel differs from the others in that, instead of a straight edge, the overlap has to be dressed around the round tubes of the top chassis and uprights X1 and X2. This can quite easily be done with a hard rubber, nylon or hide hammer. It is best, though, to first seal and rivet the panel along the bottom rear tube V, since when the aluminium is dressed around the round tube it is almost impossible to remove without damage.

ON-BOARD PANELS

On the underside front of the chassis

Fig. 12.14. The front underside panel riveted in place.

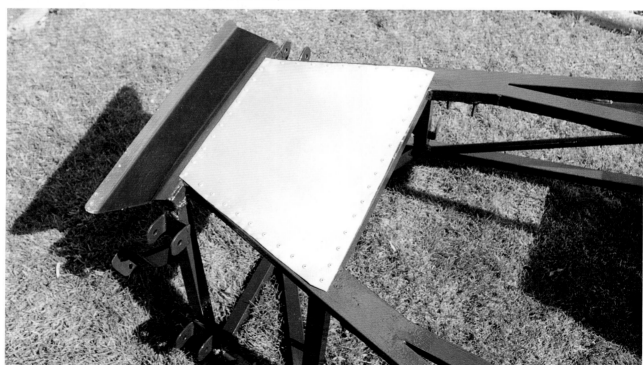

between the side chassis tubes and tubes LD and E, an aluminium panel should be riveted to help with the airflow through the radiator and to prevent road dirt and wet entering the engine bay (see *Figs. 12.14* and *12.15*). Offcuts of aluminium sheet can be used for this.

One piece of aluminium can be cut and riveted to the top of the passenger's footwell between tubes P and Q. Leave the driver's footwell uncovered at this stage for installation of the control pedal assembly. An aluminium panel needs to be made for the transmission tunnel top, but this should be secured with self-tapping screws, or bolts and captive nuts, to ease removal for maintenance work on the propshaft and handbrake (see *Fig. 12.16*).

Fig. 12.15. The front underside panel seen from above.

Fig. 12.16. Captive nuts positioned along transmission tunnel top rails for fixing a removable panel.

SCUTTLE/BULKHEAD

Cut 1in (25mm) square tube identical to chassis tube P, and clamp on top of chassis tube P with G-clamps. Then cut two 1in (25mm) square tubes to fit from P to the ends of tubes H where they join tubes N. Tack weld the three tubes together, remove from chassis and fully weld. Mark the top and grind or file off the raised weld bead on the underside to present a flat surface to the chassis. Now attach with G-clamps a piece of 16swg mild steel 37.9in (963mm) wide by 10in (254mm) high to the front edge of the long tube, flush with the bottom, and weld in place. The corners must be radiused in the same way as the dashboard (see plan). A strip of ½in x ⅛in (13mm x 3mm) mild steel must also be tack welded, edge on, around the front edge ⅛in (3mm) below the extreme edge of the bulkhead panel. This becomes the rear bonnet support strip.

For the next stage it will help to obtain a piece of blockboard or plywood measuring 42in x 12in (1.1m x 305mm). Cut the top edge to the shape of the dashboard with radiused corners (see plan). Now bend a strip of ½in x ⅛in (13mm x 3mm) steel strip to this outline, and weld the strip in place at an angle of 60 degrees. If necessary, tack weld in two or three temporary stays to hold the shape and angle.

Cut seven 2in (50mm) lengths from a 1in x ⅛in (25mm x 3mm) steel strip, then weld in position. These brackets will secure the scuttle to the chassis either by welding or by 10mm bolts and Rivnuts (devices for inserting threads in tube or sheet material).

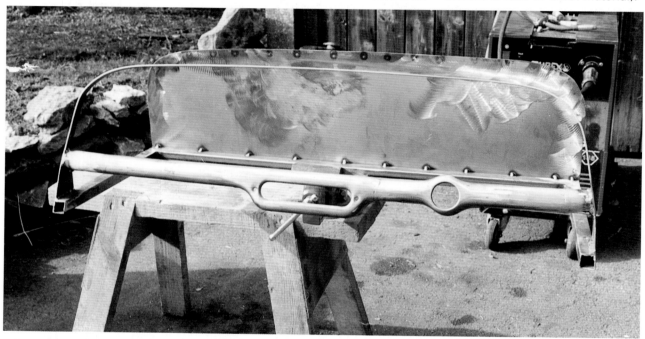

Fig. 12.17. A scuttle in process of construction. This one incorporates a cross member from a Mini.

Fig. 12.18. Front view of mild steel panel cut and welded on to framework to form scuttle.

Cut to fit a length of 1in (25mm) square tube and weld in place using the dashboard pattern as a guide.

The final stage is to make a card pattern of the outside skin, lay it on an aluminium sheet and cut out and fit in the manner described. Alternatively, you could make it from 20swg steel and weld it on.

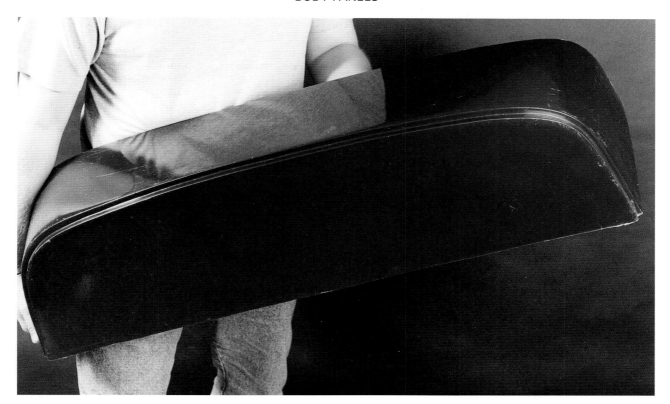

Fig. 12.19. The scuttle can also be made of glassfibre, as this example. (Photo. Steve Williams)

Fig. 12.20. A scuttle panel in place, showing mounting brackets welded to the scuttle rail and secured in position on the chassis by Rivnuts, bolts and spring washers.

BONNET

With your nose cone secured in place, the chassis panelled and your dashboard/bulkhead fitted, cover the whole area where the bonnet will lay with one piece of thin card, overlapping 1in. If this is held tightly in place with tape it will take on a perfect bonnet shape without a ripple or blemish. With your finger tip or thumbnail you will be able to feel the outline shape of the bulkhead, bonnet support lip and the nose cone support lip. With a soft pencil, trace these outlines. To trace the bonnet sides I found it easier to make an indentation by running my thumbnail along these edges.

Take the card off and, allowing an extra 1in at the sides for later folding under, cut out your pattern

with scissors. Transfer the pattern to aluminium sheet and cut out with tin snips. Place the cut out aluminium sheet over the bonnet area and curve it over by hand to take up the bonnet shape. Another pair of hands helps, and between you it is possible to form the bonnet curvature entirely without special tools. When everything is

bent to shape, tape the sides in place. You should have a 1in (25mm) overlap on both sides.

Check the gap on the nose cone and bulkhead. It should be between 1/16in (1.5mm) and 1/8in (3mm) evenly at both ends. If there is an overlap you may have to very carefully mark and retrim with the tin snips.

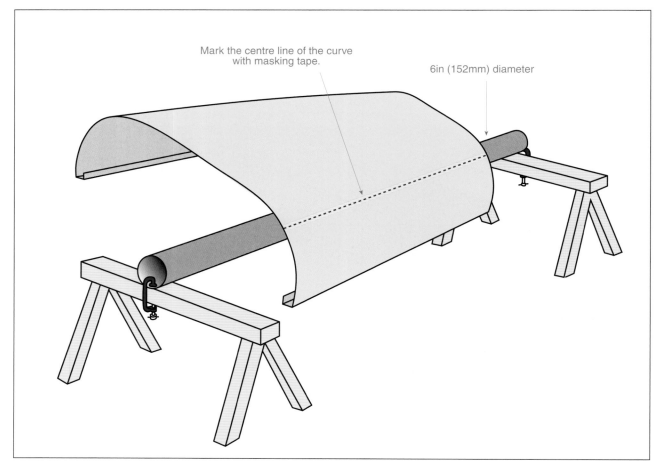

Mark the centre line of the curve
with masking tape.

6in (152mm) diameter

Fig. 12.21. This method of bending the bonnet is included courtesy of Peter Dunn. Secure the 6in diameter plastic pipe to the two 'horses' with G-clamps, and use your hands to bend the aluminium sheet over the pipe. It's a good idea to recruit a second pair of hands for this job.

Fig. 12.22. If the SVA inspector queries your bonnet catches, here's a way of dealing with the problem.

Finally, with the bonnet still taped in place and the chassis supported on axle stands, get underneath and mark along tubes J1 and J2 on the inside of the bonnet with a soft pencil. Remove the tape and take off the bonnet. You may decide to readjust the pencil lines to give 1/16in (1.5mm) to 1/8in (3mm) gap on bonnet sides. Fold inwards over two pieces of softwood as previously described, and your bonnet is now complete and can be secured with four catches.

Cutting and shaping louvres is a long job. If you really want them, you first need to mark them out, then drill four 1/16in (1.5mm) holes close together at the start of each louvre so that these can be filed together into a slot big enough to get a hacksaw blade into. Then cut along the marked line and shape the louvre by using pliers. This is rather a crude way of doing the job compared with the carved wooden former (or mould) and panel beater's hammer that a professional would use, but we are trying to keep costs down.

PAINTING

If you have got to this stage of the panelling with no marks, dents or other blemishes, I think the car should be left unpainted. Polished aluminium looks good, and all you

Fig. 12.23. A panel-beater's special wooden former for use in making louvres. (Photo. Steve Williams)

Fig. 12.24. The bonnet, hand-formed from one piece of 18 gauge aluminium (using the scuttle and nose cone as formers) showing the hand-cut louvres.

Fig. 12.25. Nose cone, scuttle and bonnet – trial fitting.

need is a tin of metal polish and a few soft rags.

However, if you have used salvaged aluminium sheet you may have no alternative but to paint. Aluminium must first be etch primed with special primer, or whatever topcoat you use will flake off in time.

After the etch primer has dried, flat it down with 1000 grit wet and dry paper, taking care not to rub back to bare aluminium. Then spray on two or three coats of your chosen colour of topcoat. When fully dried, cut back with metal polish and apply a coat of wax for a showroom finish.

PART 4

PUTTING EVERYTHING TOGETHER

CHAPTER 13

Final assembly

Now that you have made and obtained all the parts and materials required for your Locost you have, in effect, a collection of parts very similar to the contents of a kit you could have purchased from one of the kit-car manufacturers. The next stage is final assembly.

STEERING RACK
The steering rack is attached to the chassis by the two mounting clamps which you bolt to the special brackets previously welded to the frame for this purpose, and the track rods will eventually connect, by way of the track rod ends, to the steering arm on the uprights (front hub assemblies) which are attached to your suspension wishbones.

Depending on the engine and gearbox combination used, the weight on the front wheels can vary +50lb (23kg) or –50lb (23kg). To accommodate this the position of the steering rack can be raised or lowered a little.

Your aim should be to have the steering rack and track rod parallel to the ground with the vehicle at its final weight. If this is achieved you will have precise and stable steering. If the track rods are not

Fig. 13.1. A pre-panelling kit layout of chassis, front and rear suspension components, nose cone and mudguards in readiness for assembly.

Fig. 13.2. Ford Escort steering rack in situ, painted and fitted with new rubber bellows. In this case a Ford sticker was applied after painting. The steering coupling shown here is from the donor Escort.

Fig. 13.3. Steering track rod linked up to steering arm on wheel upright.

parallel you will have a characteristic known as 'bump steer'. As the car rises and falls whilst travelling over road undulations, this causes the distance between the track rod ends to shorten and lengthen making the vehicle toe-in and toe-out and causing it to wander slightly. Do not worry unduly about this; I have driven factory produced cars which have this problem, and most drivers do not seem to notice it.

ENGINE AND GEARBOX MOUNTING

The steel engine mounting plates will be positioned between rails F1 and G1 and between F2 and G2 on the space frame, and their exact location will depend on your chosen engine.

It is important for adequate ground clearance that the engine sump does not hang below the bottom chassis rail by more than 1in (25mm). The method I have used many times is to support the chassis on a flat surface with 1in (25mm) thick pieces of wood or metal. Then, if you have proper lifting gear, lower the engine and gearbox unit into position in the chassis, with the sump coming to rest on the ground. However, the popular way is to lower the chassis over the engine, but if you do it this way you will first need to remove the alternator.

Place the engine as far back as possible and make sure that you will have sufficient clearance for the clutch release arm through its range of movement and that all the ancillaries (distributor, exhaust manifold, carburettor, etc.) clear the chassis and the intended route of the steering column. In particular, ensure that the starter motor has a good half-inch clearance from the chassis, and see that the gearbox is centrally located at the head of the transmission tunnel. The standard Ford Escort gearbox mount can be used, slightly narrowed to fit into the transmission tunnel.

You can now establish the exact

position for your engine mounting brackets and the gearbox mounts. Having marked these, lift the chassis from the engine and weld on the engine mounting brackets, and make gearbox mountings by welding on short lengths of ¾in (19mm) RHS as shown in *Fig. 13.6.* Be sure to cap the ends of the RHS supports to keep them watertight. The gearbox support can then be welded in place.

Now refit the engine and gearbox and connect the front end of the propshaft.

Fig. 13.4. Offside engine mounting bracket welded in place.

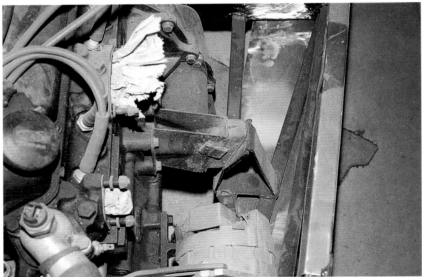

Fig. 13.5. A nearside view of engine mounted on bracket, incorporating the rubber bush.

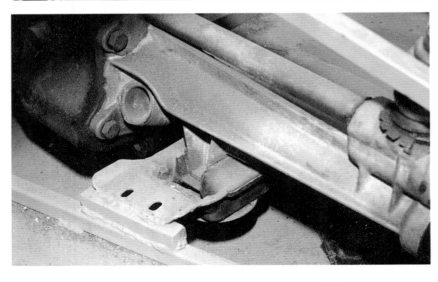

Fig. 13.6. A nearside view of the gearbox mounting.

FRONT SUSPENSION ASSEMBLY

Bolt the bottom wishbones in position, having lightly coated the bolts in copper grease. Be sure you use a flat washer under each bolt head and a locking nut. Bolt the bottom swivel joints on to the bottom wishbones. Screw the top swivels on to the top wishbones, making sure the lock nuts are fitted, then bolt to the chassis as described for the bottom wishbones. Check that it is the correct way up, as if the wishbones are fitted incorrectly the castor angle will be affected.

Next, fix in place the Cortina uprights, hubs and brake assemblies. If correctly fitted the brake calipers will be at the rear. Bolt the front shock absorbers to the top chassis mountings (again using copper grease). Now raise

Fig. 13.7. Diagrams showing the castor angle, camber angle and toe-in.

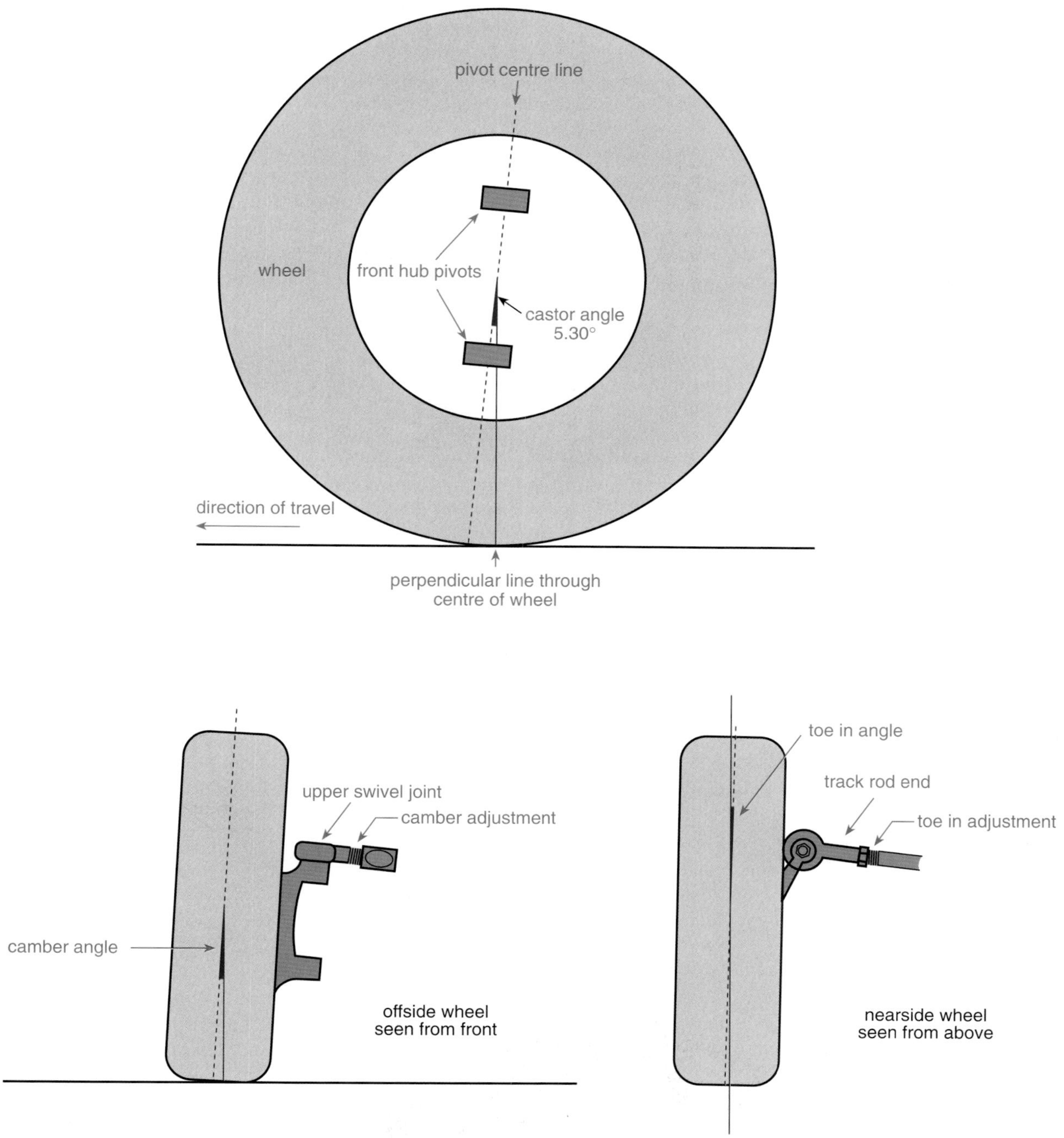

the suspension to bolt the shock absorber bottom mountings to the bottom wishbones.

Attach the track rod ends to the Cortina steering arms. Fit the front wheels and you can now move your chassis about like a wheelbarrow.

The camber angles and toe-in can be set at your local tyre depot, but the castor angle is fixed by the chassis and wishbone design. For this reason it is a good idea, when first assembling all the front suspension (including shock absorbers, wheels and tyres), to just tack weld the suspension brackets in place (see Chapter 4) and recheck positioning against the drawings for accuracy before dismantling and finally welding the brackets in place. Camber angle can be altered by adjusting the upper swivel joints, and toe in is determined by adjusting the track rod ends.

So, the correct castor angle will automatically be achieved if your brackets are accurately positioned. For information, it should be 5.30° but a variation of ±0.3° is also acceptable.

REAR SUSPENSION ASSEMBLY

Rest the rear axle in the chassis. Assemble the springs on to the shock absorbers and bolt them to the mountings on the axle. Raise the axle, insert the propshaft into the differential and bolt the shock absorbers to the chassis. Allow the axle to hang on the shock absorbers. Fit the four trailing arms and the Panhard rod. Raise the chassis and fit the road wheels. You now have a rolling chassis.

STEERING COLUMN

At this stage the steering column can be fitted and measurements taken for the extension shaft (see Chapter 5). Fabricate the shaft with care and, unless you are an expert welder, get your work checked over by a specialist. Remember what has been said about ensuring that your column/shaft arrangement will deflect or absorb the energy

from a head-on collision. The next step is to establish the steering wheel position to best suit the driver, and then to weld in place a supporting RHS crossmember across the scuttle frame, on to which a bracket should be welded at the appropriate place. It is on to this bracket that the steering column tube is bolted. To secure the crossmember a triangular piece

of steel must be welded on to the scuttle frame on each side.

Naturally, you will have to cut a hole in the scuttle panel for the steering column to pass through, and its position will depend on your preferences. Once the column is mounted, the extension shaft can be fitted to the column shaft and the steering rack by way of the universal joints.

Fig. 13.8. Sit in the rolling chassis and establish the most comfortable position for the steering wheel before making up your mounting bracket.

Fig. 13.9. A hole cut in the scuttle panel for the steering column.

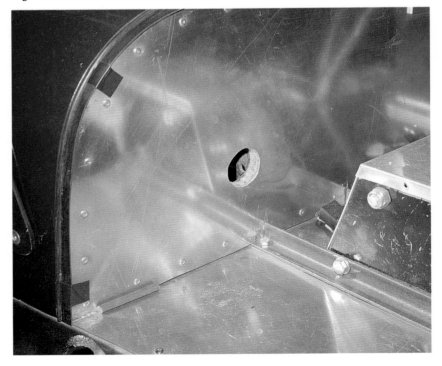

Fig. 13.10. A steering column in situ.

EXHAUST SYSTEM

With the engine in place, the exhaust manifold can be fitted, along with the rest of the exhaust system (see Chapter 9).

RADIATOR AND FAN ASSEMBLY

Bolt the radiator and electric fan in position on the mounting brackets (see Chapter 4). You will have to connect the top outlet of the radiator to the Fiesta thermostat housing that you fitted to the engine and the bottom outlet to the water pump with suitable hoses with the correct bends. How your fan is fitted will depend on the sort that you have acquired (see Chapter 9).

At this point, check everything over thoroughly to be sure that your alignments and positioning are correct. Having seen that all is well, dismantle what you have done and fully weld any chassis brackets where only tack welds have been made. Also, make sure all your welds are cleaned up before giving the chassis its final coat of paint. The paint you use is, of course, your choice. Use two coats of primer and two coats of colour on top of the previously applied rust-inhibiting paint, but take advice on whether the paints are compatible, or test on a piece of scrap steel.

Once the paint is dry, replace the engine and reassemble all but for the front wishbone suspension and hub units.

Fig. 13.11. Showing an electric fan and radiator in position.

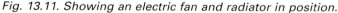

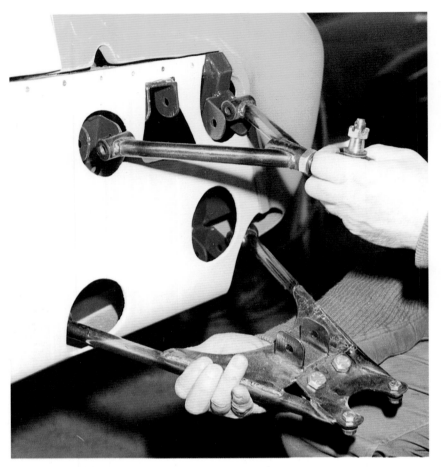

BODY PANELS

Now is the time to fit the body panels, or you could do this prior to reassembly – it is a matter of choice. The illustrations in Chapter 12 are of the pre-assembly method, as what needs to be done is more clearly shown this way. Accessibility is the benefit, but the disadvantage is that unless you are very careful you will quite likely damage the aluminium panelling during installation of the engine, propshaft, rear axle and suspension.

Panelling after assembly calls for putting the car up on stands so that you can reach underneath, and naturally the front suspension units cannot be attached to the chassis until you have fitted the front side panels.

Fig. 13.12. When reassembling the front suspension units, make sure that the wishbones can move freely up and down without fouling the body panels.

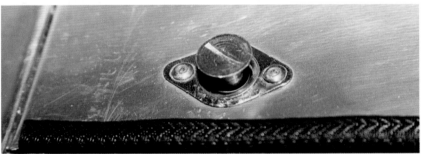

Fig. 13.13. A Dzus fastener pop riveted to an aluminium panel. (Photo. Steve Williams)

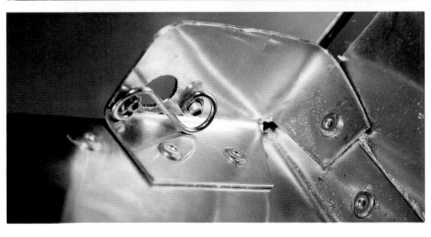

Fig. 13.14. A Dzus fastener spring clip pop riveted to a bracket. (Photo. Steve Williams)

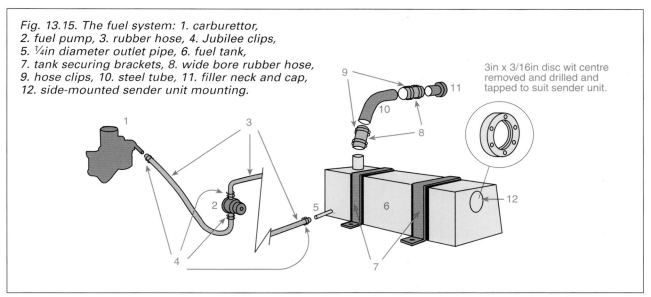

Fig. 13.15. The fuel system: 1. carburettor, 2. fuel pump, 3. rubber hose, 4. Jubilee clips, 5. ¼in diameter outlet pipe, 6. fuel tank, 7. tank securing brackets, 8. wide bore rubber hose, 9. hose clips, 10. steel tube, 11. filler neck and cap, 12. side-mounted sender unit mounting.

3in x 3/16in disc wit centre removed and drilled and tapped to suit sender unit.

FUEL TANK FITTING

Secure the fuel tank by the two fabricated steel straps made from mild steel strip 1in (25mm) wide and ⅛in (3mm) thick. It is essential, after painting them, to stick ⅛in (3mm) rubber strips on the inside, and on the chassis rails where the tank sits, to insulate it from vibration and wear. If you are fitting a fuel gauge you must provide a secure earth wire to the chassis, as the rubber strips will also insulate the tank electrically. The securing straps are best fixed to the chassis rails by Rivnuts and bolts which provide a strong but removable fixing.

See Chapter 10 on the fuel tank for information on fitting the fuel gauge sender unit.

Fig. 13.16. The fuel tank in situ.

Fig. 13.17. Shows a fuel tank retaining strap and rubber. And yes, we do know the shock absorber is upside down!

Fig. 13.18. When fitting the fuel filler cap ensure you leave adequate clearance for the spare wheel to be mounted centrally on the rear panel.

Fig. 13.19. SVA regulations are that such items as filler caps must not stand more than 50mm proud of the surface of the car. No problem with this flush-fitting lockable cap. (Photo. Steve Williams)

HANDBRAKE ASSEMBLY

The Escort handbrake is bolted on to the mountings in the transmission tunnel, and the rubber gaiter from the donor car can be reused.

You now need to fit the pair of Austin Allegro handbrake cables, securing the cable outers to fabricated brackets welded in position on the rear axle casing and on the transmission tunnel.

Fig. 13.20. Handbrake cable bracket made from a piece of angle iron. This needs to be welded in position under the top rails of the transmission tunnel.

Fig. 13.21. Handbrake cables leading to rear wheels.

Fig. 13.22. Handbrake cable mounting bracket welded to back axle casing.

MASTER CYLINDER AND BRAKE PIPES

A split or dual circuit brake system with red failure-warning light is a requirement of SVA regulations. No problem if your donor car already has one. Mount the servo unit and dual master cylinder on the footwell panel in a central position as high as possible, and fit the fluid reservoir, ensuring accessibility. Fit the pedal assembly on to the pedal cross-shaft. It may be necessary to redrill the hole for the clevis pin securing the master cylinder pushrod if the pedal has been raised or lowered to suit the driver. However, always use a new split pin of the correct size.

The location for the pedal return springs and brake light switch (salvaged from the original pedal box) can easily be manufactured from scrap and fixed to the bulkhead.

Now, attach three flexible brake pipes (one for each front caliper and one for the rear axle mounting) on to the brake pipe brackets welded to the chassis at the appropriate points (see *Fig. 4.1*). Secure each with a spring washer and locknut. Attach a three-way brake pipe union to the back axle casing and connect up the flexible pipe. Then, at the front wheels, connect the two flexible pipes to the calipers, remembering the copper washers between brake pipes and calipers. Using a Rivnut and bolt, secure a three-way union in a convenient place at the front of the chassis.

It is now time to make and fit the rigid pipework. The cost of steel or long-lasting copper alloy brake pipe is sufficiently low to justify making all new pipes. If you do not have a brake pipe flaring tool, you can cut your pipe to the correct lengths and get a garage to flare the ends for you. Alternatively, most good car accessory shops will supply brake pipes to your measurements with the ends already flared. Familiarise yourself with which ends of the pipe should be 'male' and which 'female' (see *Fig. 13.28*).

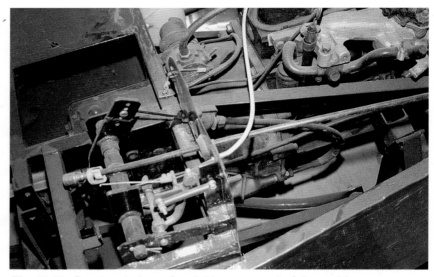

Fig. 13.23. Overhead view of pedal box cross-shaft in position.

Make two brake pipes for the rear axle and fix in place with existing brake pipe securing tabs. Make brake pipes to run from the nearside front and offside front brakes to the three-way brake pipe junction, securing in place with P-clips riveted to the chassis rails, adhesive pipe clips or cable ties. Be sure that they do not come in contact with any moving parts, like the steering column. Make one long brake pipe from the three-way junction to one of the two unions on the dual master cylinder, again fixing securely. Then run another long pipe from the other master cylinder union, along the inside of the transmission tunnel (keeping away from the propshaft, handbrake and linkages, etc.) to connect to the flexible pipe at the

Fig. 13.24. Shows modified pedal assembly and attachment points for master cylinder push rods. The pedals will have to be redrilled to move the clevis pins from the original position.

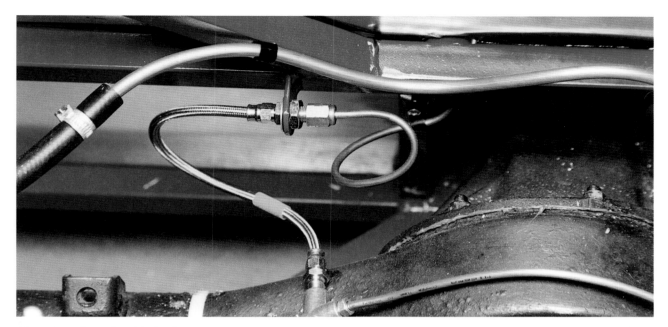

Fig. 13.25. Rear flexible brake piping fitted to the chassis and rear axle casing by means of brackets welded in place. (Photo. Steve Williams)

Fig. 13.26. Front brake pipe mounting bracket, and showing both rigid and flexible piping in place. Note: The rigid piping has yet to be clipped to the chassis.

chassis bracket just above the rear axle. Make sure that the pipes are fixed tightly to the chassis to prevent movement and possible damage.

This is a front/rear split system. An alternative is a diagonal split which divides the system between nearside rear/offside front and offside rear/nearside front (see *Fig. 13.28*), but this will call for flexible pipes to be used on each rear wheel.

Finally, when everything is connected up, fill the system with brake fluid and carry out the bleeding procedure in the normal way.

Fig. 13.27. A brake pipe flaring kit. A useful addition to your tool collection, but it can easily be hired by the day. (Photo. Steve Williams)

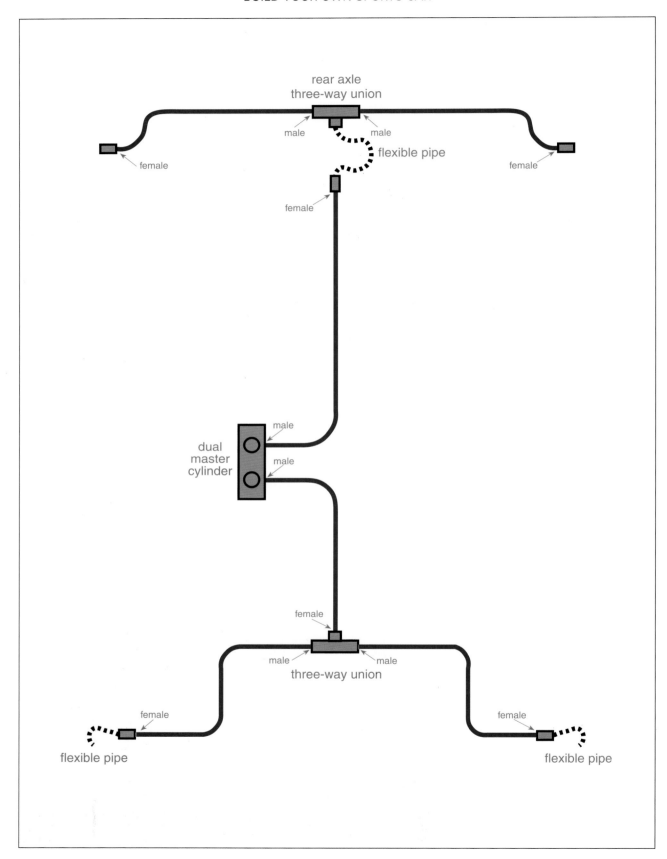

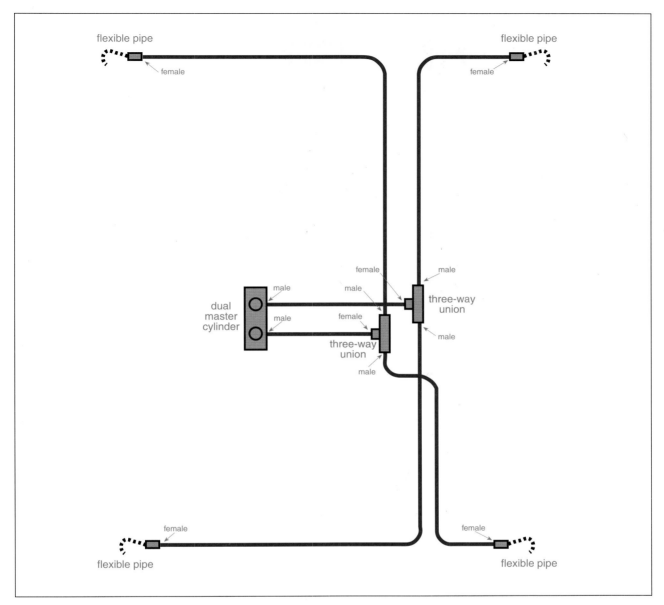

Fig. 13.28. Plans of rigid and flexible brake piping for a split or dual system – front and rear (opposite) and diagonal arrangements (above).

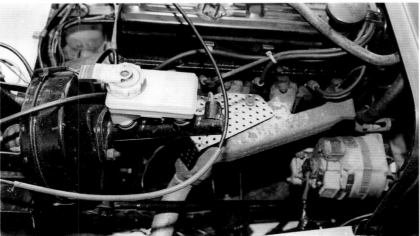

Fig. 13.29. An Escort dual master cylinder with brake fluid level warning light fitting, attached to servo unit. (Photo. Steve Williams)

Fig. 13.30. A brake pipe running along the near side of the transmission tunnel. On the right is the fuel pipe. Also shows the handbrake mounting bracket. (Photo. Steve Williams)

FIXING GLASS FIBRE MUDGUARDS AND NOSE CONE

The nose cone is held in position with Dzus fasteners so that it is easily removed for access to the radiator, steering rack, fan, horn, etc.

Make sure that the radiator opening in the nose cone is not obstructed by the number plate or badges as it is essential for effective cooling to get as much air through as possible.

The rear mudguards should be held in position by a helper while holes are drilled through the mounting flange and the aluminium body panel. They can then be bolted on with small nuts and bolts and large washers either side to spread the load. It is a nice touch to sandwich plastic beading between body and wings. This can be bought in various colours from good trim shops, or it can be salvaged from scrap vehicles.

The front cycle wings are secured to the front uprights so that they turn and move up and down with the wheels. Make the stays from ¾in (19mm) steel tube and steel strip as shown in the plan. Each wing is then drilled and bolted on with four small nickel-plated coach bolts.

Fig. 13.32. Made-up front wing stays (nearside on left and offside on right). For each front wheel the drilled bracket which connects the two arms fits under the top swivel joint, and the bottom bracket is secured by one of the caliper bolts.

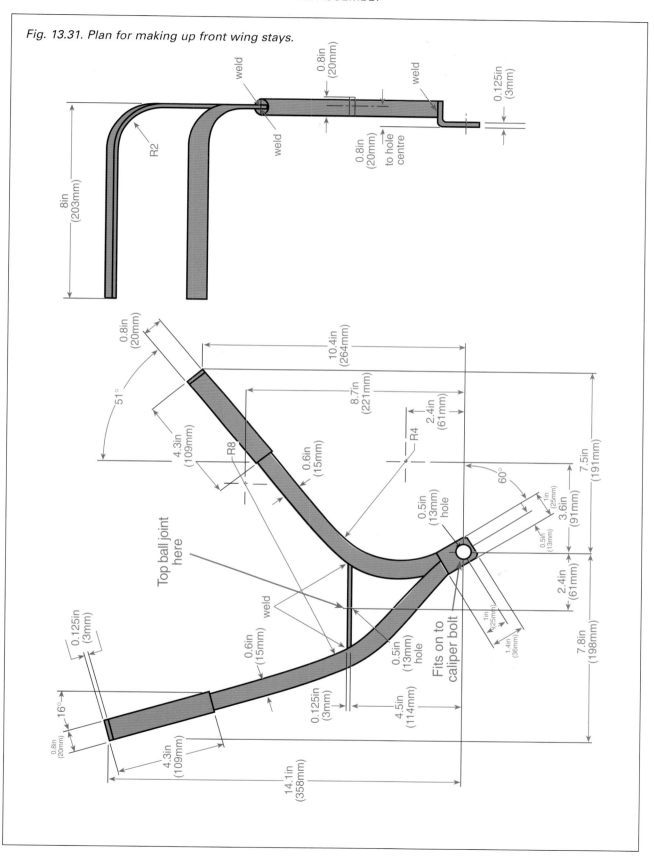

Fig. 13.31. Plan for making up front wing stays.

Fig. 13.33. A front wing stay in position.

DASHBOARD/INSTRUMENTS

Cut out the dashboard from ⅛in (3mm) thick aluminium sheet to the pattern shown in *Fig. 13.34*, suitably scaled up. First, cut it slightly larger, then grind or sand it down to make a perfect fit to the scuttle. The layout of the instruments can be to your own choice.

Next, apply some form of foam padding before covering in vinyl (so that your instrument bezels can be recessed) and fit to the scuttle with 12 self-tapping screws and cup washers. Finish off with plastic edging around the outside edge (see *Fig. 13.35*).

The standard instrument assembly from your donor Escort can be used, mounting it directly on to your Locost dashboard with a suitable area cut out to clear the back of the assembly and speedo cable. This has the distinct advantage of being readily available, and the existing loom will clip straight back on as it was originally.

Fig. 13.34. Dashboard pattern. The positioning of the instruments and switches is your own choice, of course.

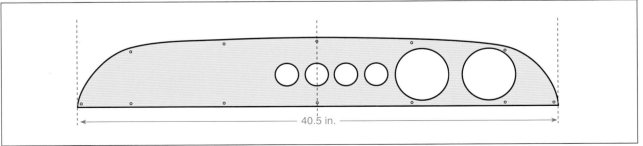

40.5 in.

Fig. 13.35. A padded and edged dashboard on a finished SVA-passed Locost. (Photo. Steve Williams)

Fig. 13.36. A registration number rear backing plate with number plate light attached. (Photo. Steve Williams)

REAR NUMBER PLATE AND SPARE WHEEL CARRIER

Cut out a backing plate for the car's registration number from ¹⁄₁₆in (1.6mm) steel sheet, making provision for the number plate light (see *Fig. 13.36*). Bend a length of ¾in (19mm) tube as shown in *Fig. 13.37*, and weld on two pieces of ⅛in (3mm) steel strip on to which the backing plate is fitted (as shown). Weld the tubular arms on to the chassis frame, allowing space to accommodate the spare wheel of your car (see *Fig. 13.38*, although in this case the builder has welded on pinch clamps to allow for adjustment).

Fig. 13.37. A spare wheel carrier and rear number plate assembly. (Photo. Steve Williams)

Fig. 13.38. Rear number plate and spare wheel carrier in situ.

ELECTRICAL EQUIPMENT
Wiring loom
It helps to find a large flat surface upon which you can spread the loom out. You will see that it is in two sections.

The rear loom, running from behind the facia to the rear lights should be secured inside the Locost transmission tunnel with P-clips or cable ties, taking care to avoid moving parts like the propshaft, axle or handbrake. It will contain wires for the fuel tank sender unit (green/black), rear number plate light (red/orange), rear lamps, stop lamps and direction indicator lamps, all with their own codes. It is a simple matter to attach the wires to the correct units. In most cases the wires will need shortening, which entails cutting off to the correct length, stripping the insulation back ¼in (6mm) and crimping on a new terminal end with a special crimping tool.

I have not had a problem with the wires being too short, but if a wire should need lengthening it is best to solder on another piece with the same colour coding obtained from another Escort in a scrapyard. Make sure the soldered joint is well insulated with tape.

You will find you have a lot of spare wires left over – such as the ones which were connected to items like door courtesy light switches, cigar lighter, etc. Since your car does not require such refinements you can simply remove them from the loom and retape the end.

An alternative is to entirely dismantle the Escort wiring loom, select the wires that you need and make up a new loom of your own.

If your donor car did not have a rear fog light you will need to wire one in (don't connect it to the brake light circuit), and it is a requirement to fit a warning light that is visible from the driving seat. Likewise, if you fit a reversing light this too must have a warning light inside the car unless it is switched on by the selection of reverse gear.

You will also need to wire in direction indicator repeaters to each side of the car, linking them in to the front and rear indicator circuit. And, the hazard warning light circuit must be independent of the ignition switch.

Be sure to use grommets to prevent chafing where the loom passes through panels. If you did not remove them from the Escort, grommets can be purchased in different sizes for just a few pence. Secure all wires with cable ties.

WIRING DIAGRAM KEY
(See *Fig. 13.39*)
You may not need every one of these wires on your car. Just ignore those that are not required.

1 Hazard switch
2 Heater switch
3 Dash light switch
4 Rear fog switch
5 Wiper switch
6 Washer switch
7 Spare
8 Head lights switch
8a Rear fog light switch
9 Indicator switch
10 Ignition switch
11 Choke warning
12 Fuel Gauge
13 Water temperature gauge
14 Engine oil warning
15 Rev counter
16 Main beam warning
17 Speedometer
18 Ignition warning
19 Oil pressure gauge
20 Battery volts
21 Horn push
22 Main/dip switch
23 Indicator l/h front
24 Headlight l/h
25 Sidelight l/h front
26 Sidelight r/h front
27 Headlight right
28 Indicator r/h front
29 Water temp switch
30 Cooling fan
31 Horn
32 Horn relay
33 Battery
34 Start relay
35 Alternator
36 Water temperature
37 Distributor
38 Washer motor
39 Starter motor
40 Oil pressure switch
41 Ignition coil
42 Flasher unit
43 Wiper motor
44 Fuse box
45 Hazard unit
46 Reversing switch
47 Brake switch
48 Choke switch
49 Fuel tank
50 Number plate light
51 Indicator l/h rear
52 Stop/tail l/h
53 Reversing light
54 Rear fog light
55 Stop/tail r/h
56 Indicator r/h rear
57 Side repeater l/h
58 Side repeater r/h
59 Fog light (rear)

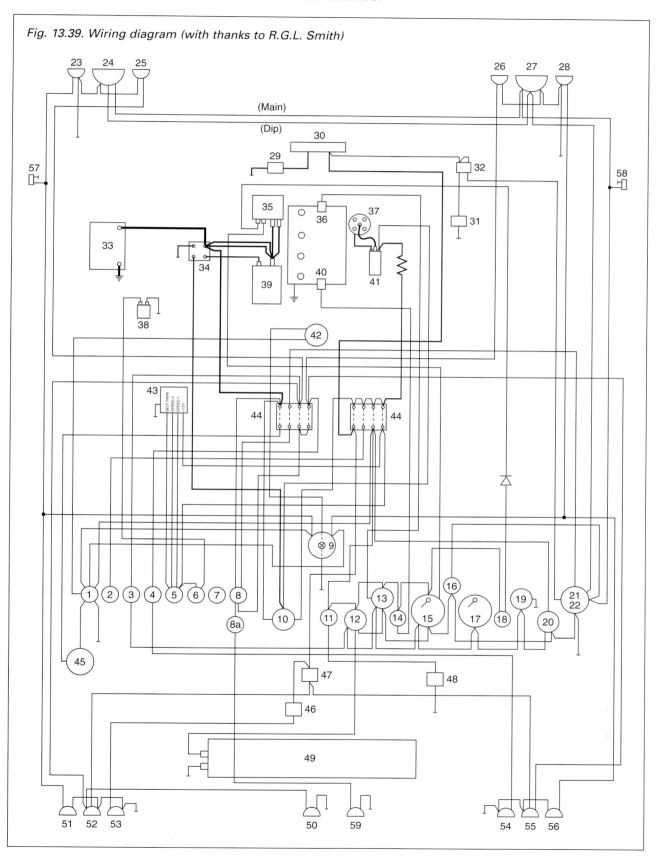

Fig. 13.39. Wiring diagram (with thanks to R.G.L. Smith)

Lights

For information on vehicle lighting regulations, including European type-approved lamps, required visibility and siting limitations, etc., see the latest copy of the *SVA Inspection Manual*.

The headlights can be fixed to a crossbar made from a piece of heavy-gauge steel tube mounted on the front chassis rails by using two brackets formed from ¾in x ⅛in (19mm x 3mm) steel offcuts and secured by four Rivnuts and bolts (see *Fig. 13.40*).

Fig. 13.40. A headlamp bar clamping bracket secured by bolts, spring washers and Rivnuts on the offside top chassis rail. To the left is a Dzus fastener mounting bracket for securing the bonnet.

Fig. 13.41. An example of headlamps (incorporating sidelights) and front indicators in an SVA-passed Locost.

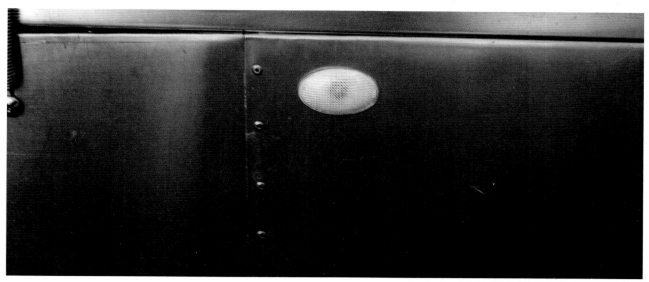

Fig. 13.42. An example of a direction indicator repeater light fitted to the side panelling at the front of the car.

Fig. 13.43. An example of rear lighting on an SVA-passed Locost.

Fig. 13.44. Close up of the sort of rear light cluster that can be used, incorporating direction indicator, reflector and position and brake lights.

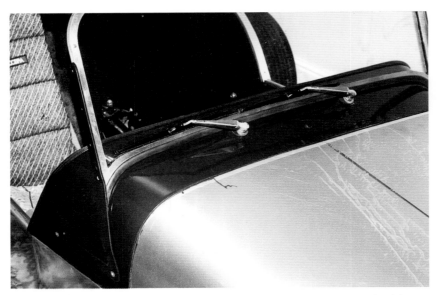

Fig. 13.45. Windscreen wipers fixed in place on the scuttle top. In this case shortened Mini wiper blades were used.

Windscreen wipers and washer

The windscreen wiper and washer assemblies that you use on your car must comply with the regulations as set out in the *SVA Inspection Manual*. The wipers can be one or two speed, but the stipulation is that they are capable of over 45 cycles per minute, and self-park out of the driver's line of view. Fitting a two-speed wiper system is probably the best bet. The wiper motor can be fitted under the scuttle on the nearside using the original bracket. Be sure to obtain the whole wiper assembly, including wiper wheel boxes and spacers. The holes in the scuttle for the wiper spindles need to be 11in (279mm) apart, 5½in (140mm) either side of the centre line and 1½in (38mm) in front of the windscreen. The tube connecting the wiper boxes will have to be shortened to fit.

The washer bottle must hold over a litre of water, and the system should be capable of clearing the screen with the wipers working. Electrically operated washers also have to pass the three- to five-second blocked nozzle test.

Horn

The horn from the donor Escort can be fitted to a radiator bracket, or anywhere else suitable under the nose cone.

Earth

Drill a hole and bolt on the engine earth lead, using a spring washer, from the engine to the chassis – a good place is the engine mounting plate.

Starter motor

It is important that the correct heavy-duty copper cables are used from the donor vehicle when wiring the starter motor circuit.

Coil

The coil should be mounted away from the exhaust pipe on a convenient chassis rail with Rivnuts, locking washers and bolts.

Fuse box

The fuse box can be mounted on the near side scuttle (engine side) without having to lengthen the wiring loom.

Brake light switch

Make a bracket to hold the brake light switch (from the donor Escort) in contact with the brake pedal. It is adjustable for length with nylon locking nuts.

Flasher unit

The flasher unit (from the donor Escort) can be secured behind the dashboard and wired into the loom.

Battery

The battery is positioned on the shelf (made from aluminium sheet) forward of the scuttle, and is held in place by 'Z' profile or angle brackets which are bolted on to the shelf and grip the lower lip of the battery casing.

Fig. 13.46. A battery in position in the engine bay, with earth strap connected.

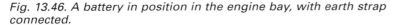

WINDSCREEN

The windscreen surround is made in two parts. The type of round-edged aluminium extrusion used in shower cubicle construction is suitable for making this up, as long as you have a means to bend it without distortion. My answer to this was a simple but very effective special tool.

First you will need to cut out a ⅜in (9mm) thick plywood template of the windscreen. The shape is given in *Fig. 13.46*, and this will need to be scaled up. Make sure that this is shaped to fit the scuttle profile and is a suitable height for the driver. Reinforce one corner with a square of 16swg steel plate on either side, and drill through both plates and plywood so that a bolt can be put through to anchor the bending tool.

The bending tool can be made up relatively easily. It is essentially two metal strips, a steel roller and a tubular handle. Assemble the finished tool on to the plywood template as illustrated, attach the aluminium extrusion and use the tool to bend it round the curve of the template.

Use the bending tool and the plywood template to form the lower part of the screen surround. To do this re-site the pivot point. Alternatively, it is possible to form the curvature of the lower part round the template by hand. Fit the two parts together and drill and tap as shown in *Fig. 13.51*. Take the completed unit, or your plywood template, to a glazier so that he can use it as a pattern to cut a piece of European type-approved 3mm laminated glass.

When fitting the glass in the surround, seal it in with silicone bath sealant.

Now screw on the screen side supports, making sure that the screws into the screen surround are not so long that they press against the glass. If they do they are almost sure to crack it. The completed screen unit can now be attached to the car, with a pliable rubber strip under the lower part of the screen surround to seal the

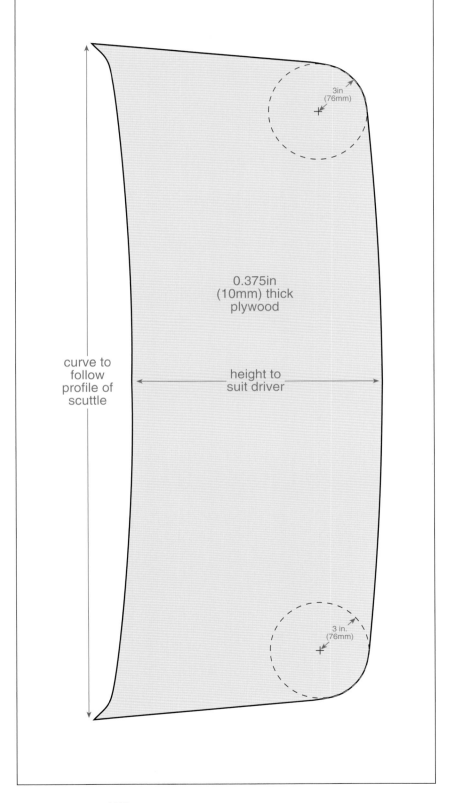

Fig. 13.47. Shape of windscreen. Scaled up, use this to cut out the plywood template.

3in (76mm)

0.375in (10mm) thick plywood

curve to follow profile of scuttle

height to suit driver

3 in. (76mm)

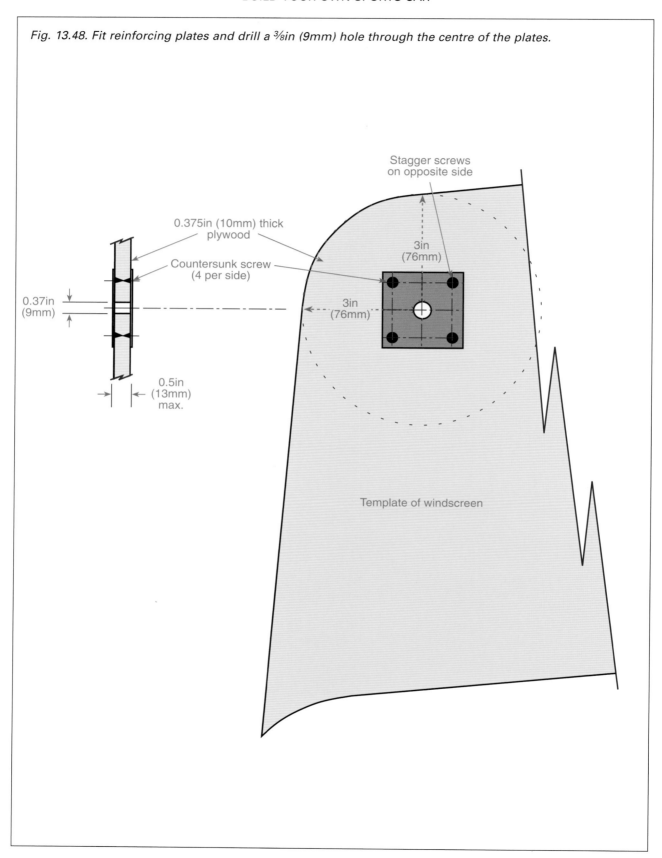

Fig. 13.48. Fit reinforcing plates and drill a ⅜in (9mm) hole through the centre of the plates.

0.375in (10mm) thick plywood

Countersunk screw (4 per side)

0.37in (9mm)

0.5in (13mm) max.

Stagger screws on opposite side

3in (76mm)

3in (76mm)

Template of windscreen

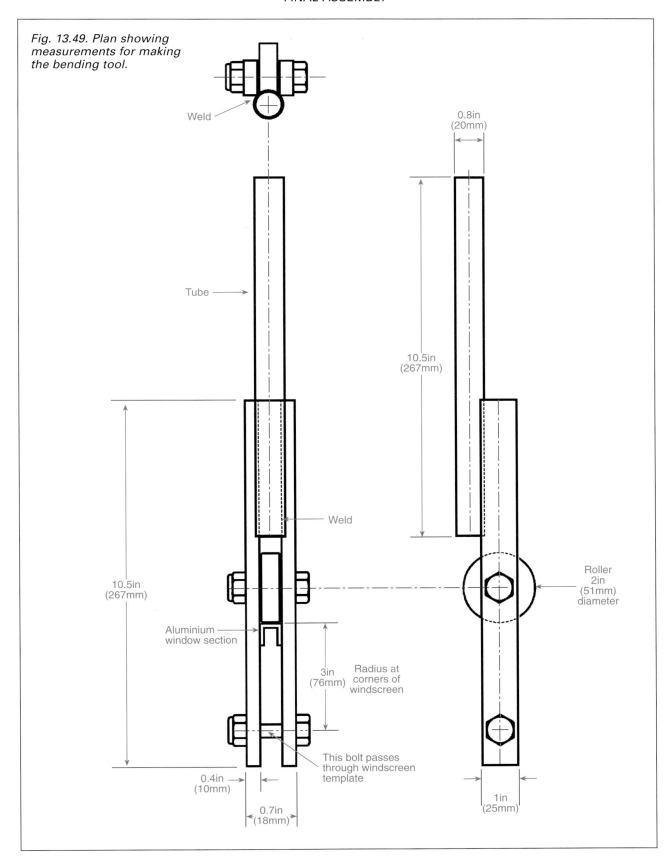

Fig. 13.49. Plan showing measurements for making the bending tool.

Weld

Tube

0.8in
(20mm)

10.5in
(267mm)

Weld

10.5in
(267mm)

Roller
2in
(51mm)
diameter

Aluminium
window section

3in
(76mm)   Radius at
corners of
windscreen

This bolt passes
through windscreen
template

0.4in
(10mm)

0.7in
(18mm)

1in
(25mm)

Fig. 13.50. Bending the aluminium extrusion takes minimal effort, and there is no distortion.

Fig. 13.51. Drill out and cut threads in the bottom part of the screen surround, then drill out the holes in the upper part one size larger to prevent screws binding.

Fig. 13.52. Plan for making windscreen side supports.

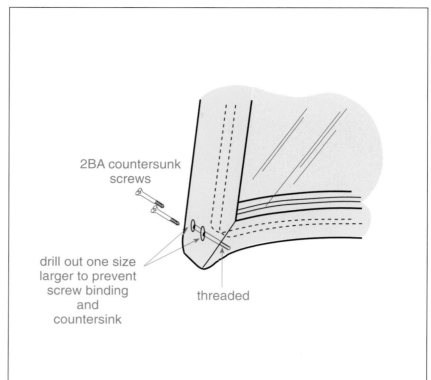

2BA countersunk screws

drill out one size larger to prevent screw binding and countersink

threaded

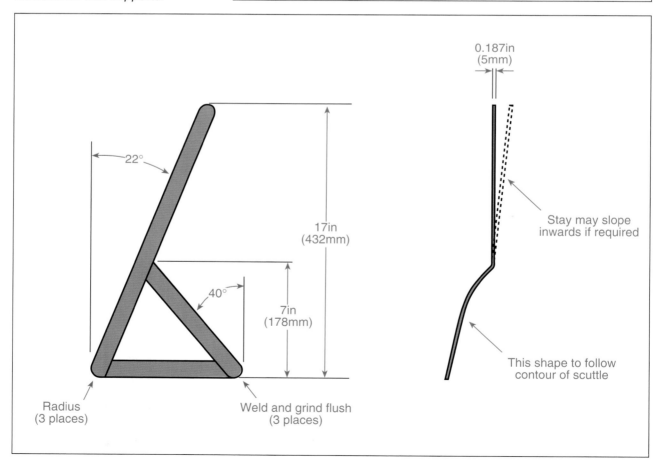

22°

0.187in (5mm)

17in (432mm)

40°

7in (178mm)

Stay may slope inwards if required

This shape to follow contour of scuttle

Radius (3 places)

Weld and grind flush (3 places)

Fig. 13.53. Windscreen side supports cut from a sheet of steel. They can also be made from three pieces of flat strip welded together. (Photo. Steve Williams)

Fig. 13.54. Windscreen surround with blunted edges. (Photo. Steve Williams)

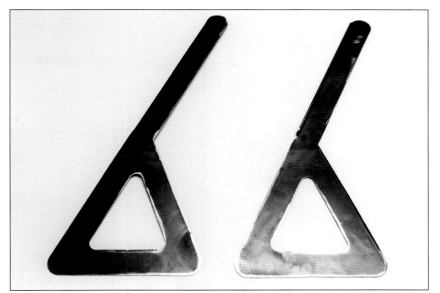

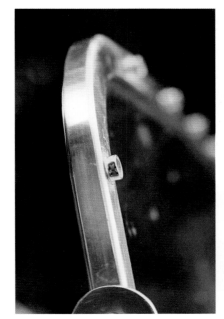

Fig. 13.55. A recycled heater/blower unit. (Photo. Steve Williams)

Fig. 13.56. A cockpit shot showing vents in the scuttle for directing warm air from the heater blower to the windscreen for demisting and defrosting.

Finished and ready to go.

screen against water seepage.

For SVA test purposes it's important to ensure that the edges of your windscreen surround are not sharp. If they are you will need to blunt them with a file. Many builders buy an approved windscreen, but this of course increases the production cost of the car.

The SVA Scheme requires that cars with full non-folding windscreens are fitted with a means of demisting and defrosting the screen

MIRRORS

The mirrors you fit to your Locost will be subject to scrutiny by the SVA test inspector. To begin with, they must be European type-approved components and they must fulfil field of view requirements. The obligatory number of mirrors is two – one on the inside and one on the outside (that is on the offside in a right-hand drive car) – but if the interior rear-view mirror doesn't afford a full view, then you will need to fit another outside mirror on the nearside.

BADGES

For a finishing touch you might like to add a badge or two. A good source is key fobs from which the metal badges can be removed and stuck on to your car in places such as the nose cone, but obviously steer clear of proprietary names.

CHAPTER 14

Interior trim and seating

All the interior panels can be made from one sheet of 8ft x 4ft (2.5m x 1.25mm) ⅛in (3mm) hardboard.

First, cut out cardboard templates with scissors, and transfer them to the hardboard. Then use a jigsaw to cut out the panels. Trial fit them to the car, adjusting where necessary. Finally, cover the panels with a vinyl of your choice, using spray-on carpet

Fig. 14.1. A rear seat as salvaged from a Van den Plas 1100.

Fig. 14.2. Shows the above seat after modification.

Fig. 14.3. A simple seat base made of ½in (13mm) plywood.

Fig. 14.4. The seat base duly completed and ready for fitting.

adhesive to hold it in place.

The panels can now be fixed to the chassis frame using self-tapping screws and cup washers every six inches.

For the seats it is possible to modify salvaged back seating from a suitable scrap car, such as a Morris 1000 Traveller where the whole back seat folds down and is plywood backed. This is what we used in my son's car, and I just jigsawed the plywood backing to fit, and cut off the surplus upholstery, leaving sufficient covering to fold around and tack to the back of the plywood. The back is held in place with five nuts and bolts. I cut the rest of the Traveller seat up to make two seat squabs and secured each to the floor with two nuts and bolts, using silicone bath sealer around the holes to prevent water getting in.

PART 5

GETTING YOUR CAR ON THE ROAD

CHAPTER 15

Legal matters

Some people seem more concerned about the legal side of producing a self-built motor car than the actual construction work. I am often asked the question: 'What if I build one and then I can't use it?' It's a fair question, but there is no single answer because every self-built car is likely to be different and, naturally, each builder/driver will be different.

For example, if you are a 17-year-old provisional licence holder and have built your own car with a 400bhp full-race Cosworth engine, then it will be extremely unlikely you will find an insurance company to provide you with cover. Likewise, if you take your vehicle for its necessary tests and the inspector feels the welding is of such poor standard as to be unsafe, then you will not pass, and rightly so. As you can see, both of these potential problems are in your control. Before any of my students started building a Locost chassis they had to satisfy me that their welding was up to the required standard.

Prior to anything else, consult a specialist insurance broker such as Footman James (see page 191) to find out the cost of cover for you and the type of vehicle and engine you have in mind.

All of the Locosts built by students in my school engineering classes had engines of 1100cc or lower. We found that this was the only way to obtain affordable insurance. All of these young builder/drivers wanted, eventually, to fit larger engines, but realised they would first have to gain experience in driving, and hoped to accrue a good record and a no claims bonus with their insurance company. As a general rule it seems that insurance becomes more affordable after you become 25 years old, especially if you have five or six years of claim-free motoring.

SINGLE VEHICLE APPROVAL SCHEME

In the UK there is now something called the Single Vehicle Approval (SVA) scheme. This is a pre-registration inspection for cars which have not been 'type-approved' to British or European standards, and it includes amateur-built cars and those using parts from previously registered vehicles. This means that you have to take your car for a pre-registration inspection at one of the relatively few SVA test stations dotted about the country. Existing heavy goods vehicle test stations are doubling up as SVA test centres.

The scheme is essentially a good one as it has the safety of you and others at heart, and it is best to view it with a positive attitude. It is, after all, only by passing the test that you will be allowed to use your car on the public roads, subject of course to the usual MoT.

The Department of the Environment, Transport and the Regions explains that the scheme's main purpose is to ensure that your car has been 'designed and constructed to acceptable safety and environmental standards'. The plan is that SVA will raise standards in both kit-cars and amateur-built cars so that they 'progressively meet the safety and environmental standards already achieved by modern production cars'. Indeed, the SVA inspection works largely to the same check-sheet that is used when production car makers put in for type-approval.

To find out exactly what will be tested, the procedures and standards that the test centre will apply and likely reasons for failure, you will need to see a copy of the Vehicle Inspectorate's *SVA Inspection Manual*. If you have to buy one, you can do so from the Inspectorate at PO Box 12, Swansea, SA1 1BP. At the time of writing the price is £25. From time to time they may offer you updating amendments for a small cost-covering sum, but once you have passed the test you may consider these of academic interest only.

At the time of writing, the cost of an SVA inspection during normal office hours is £165, and if you fail the first time you can re-submit for the reduced fee of £22 as long as you do so within three months.

Application forms can be obtained from Vehicle Registration Offices and from offices of the Vehicle Inspectorate, but you have to return the completed form, with your cheque for the fee, to the VI's Swansea office (The Vehicle Inspectorate, 91/92 The Strand, Swansea, SA1 2DH). In due course you will hear back from them with the time and place for your car's test. The test centre specified should be the one that you had chosen. The Inspectorate will also ask you for some technical details about your car – such as maximum speed and design weight – and a Vehicle Identification Number will need to be stamped somewhere on your chassis.

The SVA inspection is described as an 'engineering assessment' and it is done largely by visual checks of those parts of your car which can be seen without call for any dismantling. Naturally, the inspector will expect you to remove the bonnet. As well as the visual checks the inspector will also conduct some simple non-damaging tests on your car to make sure it complies.

It's perhaps worth saying here that the SVA test is not the equivalent of or a replacement for the MoT. Within reason, the condition of your car is outside the SVA inspector's remit.

Once the inspector is satisfied that your car meets all the design and construction regulations, you will be issued with a Minister's Approval Certificate (MAC) under SVA.

REGISTRATION

To get your Locost registered and licensed you will have to take your MAC, along with an MoT certificate and chassis number to a Vehicle Registration Office.

It's impossible to be dogmatic about the type of registration number you will be given as this seems to some extent to depend on the interpretation of your local inspector. However, if you have

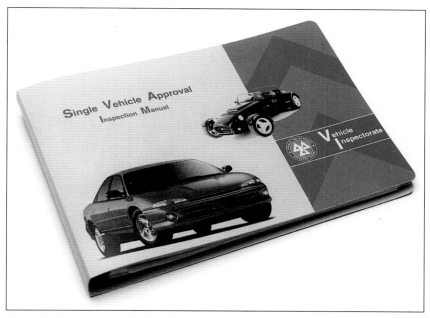

Fig. 15.1. *The Single Vehicle Approval Inspection Manual.* (Photo. Steve Williams)

built your Locost mostly from parts taken from a single donor car and can show a V5 registration document for it, the chances are that you will be given a registration number relating to the age of the donor vehicle. It may be possible for the original registration number of the donor vehicle to be retained.

On the other hand, if your car is more a compilation of parts of various origin and you do not have a V5 document for the donor car, then you will be issued with a 'Q' plate which denotes a vehicle of unknown origin.

INSURANCE

The Locost builder/owner is now able to benefit from the great number of people who build specials, kit cars and scratch-built vehicles. Special insurance companies have grown to meet the demand for insuring this type of vehicle. Unlike most other insurance companies they have specialist knowledge and are better able to calculate the risks involved. Over the years it has come to be accepted that people who build their own vehicles are amongst the

most careful drivers. Having invested hundreds of hours in the building, it is unlikely they are going to risk their pride and joy in reckless driving. These same people tend to take more care of their vehicles, too, not only from a security angle, but also in servicing and ensuring that they are always in top condition. All in all this means fewer claims and lower premiums.

Open sports cars tend to be used only in good weather, from spring to summer, so large discounts can be given for restricted mileage policies. The less the car is used the less the risk. My son's car has a policy restricting the annual mileage to 1500 miles, which is plenty for a holiday and jaunts around the countryside when the weather allows.

One of the greatest savings in insurance cost is to be made by keeping the size of the engine down. Even with a modest 1100cc Escort engine the performance is brisk and lively because of the Locost's lightness (under 1000lb). The power-to-weight ratio is excellent.

CHAPTER 16

The road test – summer 1996

The finished car was pushed out of the garage with feelings of excitement mixed with anxiety. After 12 months hard work our creation was at last ready for the use it was intended. Would it work?

We had previously run the engine for an hour at a fast tickover, regularly increasing the revs for a few minutes. With this static engine run we were able to check out the cooling system for leaks, and also the operation of the electric fan. We had to tighten all the hose clips a couple of turns as we did have several leaks – probably caused by the engine heat softening the hoses. Another check was for oil leaks, but everything seemed dry and clean. An instrument check showed that we had good oil pressure, the ammeter confirmed the dynamo was charging and the water temperature gauge was reading normal. Despite this the engine smelt very hot, though we decided that it was only the paint on the engine and exhaust manifold being baked.

When the engine had cooled, we removed the rocker cover and re-tightened the head bolts with a torque wrench, and reset the tappets (see the relevant Haynes Manual). We rechecked all nuts and bolts on the engine for tightness, but only the thermostat housing nuts needed re-tightening by half a turn.

The car at this stage did not have an MoT certificate or Road Fund licence, so could not be tested further on the public highway. Being prepared for this problem I had made arrangements to borrow a car trailer to transport our car to a local disused airfield for a test drive. We had received permission from the landowner, so the only other requirement was to obtain third party insurance, pointing out that it was for testing purposes on private land and that the vehicle did not have an MoT certificate, tax disc or number plates.

The car was loaded onto the trailer, securely lashed down, and off we set taking with us a jack, tools, oil, water, brake fluid, our first aid kit, flasks of tea and sandwiches. On the way we stopped at the local garage to fill the tank with petrol, and within minutes were surrounded by interested mechanics and passers-by, all of whom seemed to approve of what they saw, and made comments like, 'It hasn't got number plates, is it a racing car?' and 'They don't build them like that any more!'

I kept quiet as we wanted to get on our way. To tell them that we only finished building it the day before would have led to a long explanation, but I was secretly pleased that it had been mistaken for a classic sports car, because that confirmed it had just the look I had wanted to achieve with the second-hand leather on the seats and the worn wood-rimmed steering-wheel with that patina which only comes with age and use. The slightly worn chrome on the headlights, sidelights and rear lights added to the illusion. But, most of all, the smell was good – a mixture of old leather, hot oil and polish. It was a smell I knew and loved. I would never have thought it possible to recreate it, because previously I had only smelt it in vintage aircraft and genuine classic sports cars. I was glad I had packed my World War II style flying jacket and goggles!

On arrival at the airfield we came across our first problem – the barrier was down and securely padlocked, even though the previous evening the landowner had arranged to leave it open. A breakdown in communication – or had someone forgotten? My son, however, was not to be put off, and suggested that the car would go under the barrier and, at the worst, it would mean removing the windscreen (only six bolts). So we unloaded the car from the trailer, pushed it up to the barrier and, sure enough, it went under with inches to spare.

Well, this was it. Up until now the car had moved, but only by pushing or on a trailer. My son sat next to me, and my friend Graham, who had provided and driven the tow car, wished us luck. I fired the engine, checked the oil pressure and ammeter gauges, depressed the clutch, released the handbrake, selected first gear, increased the revs, released the clutch and we were away. I could hear Graham cheering as the exhaust note dropped as I changed into second. We slowed a little as we turned right onto the mile-long main runway, then into third and 40mph up the centre of the runway. I looked across to James who was wearing an enormous 'Cheshire cat' grin, then I firmly but briskly turned the steering-wheel left–right–left–right. Wow, it sticks to the tarmac like a leech, and feels very positive! Into top at 50mph, now nearing the end of the runway, then down to third then second. What a fantastic sound from the side exhaust on overrun. This is more like a racer than a sports car! A 'U' turn, and back the way we had come. It took a lot of determination not to go over our self-imposed speed limit of 50mph, as we drove back to Graham, who by this time had three cups of tea poured out. As I turned off the ignition and applied the handbrake we all started talking at once.

'It sounds fantastic!' said Graham.

'Let's have a go!' pleaded James.

I wished we had brought something stronger to celebrate with, but none the less we toasted the car with our steaming mugs of tea.

We checked for leaks. Then we checked the water, oil and brake fluid levels, and had a look round the car. When Graham noticed a dent in the nearside aluminium panelling where the exhaust exits, I realised it was where the engine had moved on its rubber mountings, either when accelerating or decelerating, causing the exhaust manifold to hit the bodywork. Naturally, over the engine and tyre noise we did not hear it. Two minutes with my tin snips put matters right, and I would touch the edges of the aluminium up with a small paint brush at home.

We now had two miles on the clock, and we decided to raise this to at least 100 miles that afternoon up and down the main runway and round and round the perimeter track. We took turns to drive and stopped every 10 miles to check the car over, constantly watching the oil pressure and water temperature.

After 65 miles James pulled in and said that there was a nasty knocking noise from the rear on right hand turns, which was getting worse. We spent the next hour removing the rear wheels, checking bearings, suspension mountings, exhaust system, tightness of rear wings etc., and we were about to give up and take the car home, to work in the comfort of our garage, when I spotted it. The green paint had been worn off just inside the rear of the transmission tunnel, about 1½in above the propshaft and differential flange. James wondered if we were going to have to widen the transmission tunnel to give a bit more clearance. I agreed and asked for the big hammer. Two well-aimed blows later, the tunnel cleared nicely. While I made a mental note to touch up the paint later, Graham asked whether I was supposed to adjust it like that. I replied that I had seen Rolls Royce panel beaters adjusting door gaps with a piece of wood and a big rubber hammer, so if it's good enough for them …

We completed 100 miles that afternoon with no further dramas. The last two runs up the runway were at 70mph and the car was as steady as an express train.

As we were loading the car back onto the trailer there was a large bang and the car would not move up the ramps any further. We looked underneath and saw that the sump was catching. We worked out that the car was 1½in lower than when we started because the springs, shock absorbers and suspension bushes had settled down. That was why the propshaft flanges were knocking. It could soon be raised up again by way of the adjustable springs, so my hammer blows proved superfluous – it didn't matter, though, as we could do with that bit of extra clearance.

The next weekend was spent resetting the ride height, changing engine oil and filter, setting the tracking, adjusting the handbrake and generally getting ready for the next hurdle – the MoT test. I sat nervously in the test centre waiting room like an expectant father, and

when the examiner came in to confirm it had passed I wished I had a cigar to give him. Instead I just thanked him, and he said it was a nice job.

On the way home I called into the Post Office, paid for the Road Fund licence and attached the tax disc to the windscreen. I knew we had really done it – built our own car. James was still having driving lessons in the family saloon and was looking forward to taking and passing his driving test. We had agreed that when he had his full licence we would both take the car to Paris for its first long run.

Over the next few months we clocked up nearly 1000 miles, with only a couple of minor problems. A leaking rocker cover gasket had covered the engine bay in oil, which meant several hours cleaning, and then the accelerator cable broke in a most inconvenient place – a main roundabout in rush hour. It was at that moment I remembered that several weeks earlier I had noticed it was fraying and had meant to change it.

James passed his test and we started planning our trip to Paris, which was to be a long weekend. Friday morning to Monday evening. It was springtime, and we were hoping for good weather as we had still not made a hood. We decided to take a few spares and tools, but we had to be careful to take only what could be packed into a plastic sandwich box as the space was very limited. We only just had room for two squashy bags, a first aid box, a small scissor jack and wheel brace and a folding warning triangle. The contents of the spares box comprised four spare bulbs, one roll of insulating tape, one metre of wire, four fuses, one Jubilee clip, one fan belt, one spark plug and a set of points. We also managed to get in four spanners, one pair of small Mole grips and a screwdriver with interchangeable tips.

The car was packed the evening before departure, all fluid levels were checked and the tyre pressures increased by a couple of lbs/sq in as all our motoring would be on motorways at near the legal limit. Although we had both been to Paris before, this trip seemed to be more of an adventure. It must be the same feeling that those early pioneer motorists had.

On Friday morning we were up at the crack of dawn, passports and ferry tickets secure in the inside pockets of our flying jackets, which were zipped up against the early morning chill. We set off on the 200 mile drive to Dover. We had estimated a little over three hours driving time, but after joining the M25 it became one of those stop/start traffic jams, and every time we stopped we had a new interested person alongside, most of whom wound down their windows to pass favourable comments. When we reached the Dartford river crossing I must have been the only driver who could not reach the cash machine, as we were so low on the ground. I stood on the seat and tossed the coins in, wriggled back down under the steering-wheel, and the next stop was Dover.

Needless to say, we missed our intended ferry and had an hour's wait. Using this time for refreshments, we selected a table by a window in the café overlooking the rapidly growing queues in the departure area. It was amusing to watch other drivers walk over to the car for a closer inspection, and I wished I could have heard their comments. I also started mentally designing a lockable lid for the luggage area! James pointed out that this was the longest run (220 miles) without stopping, and no problems (we both touched wood).

Ten minutes to loading, the Tannoy called for drivers to return to their cars. I could see the problem before it happened. The loading ramp to the ship was very steep, and at the top immediately fell away to the lower deck. Sure enough, we scraped to a halt at the top, and it felt like a plank on a see-saw. I immediately jumped out to push, but the removal of my 15-stone was enough. The suspension raised a little and, with a bit of a push from me, James drove on. Despite my

protests that it was mostly the weight of the luggage and tools causing the problem, James still suggested a diet for me to lose some weight.

It was a calm crossing and James was looking forward to his first taste of driving on the right. We were the only car to be stopped by the French Immigration Control, who checked our passports and then waved us on. I wonder why?

It was now past lunchtime and we were hungry. The fuel gauge was reading low, so we turned off the autoroute into a service area and filled up the tank. A distance of 323 miles from home on a tankful was not bad. We parked and walked back to the restaurant area, taking our bags with us (I kept thinking about a lockable lid). Over a good lunch we worked out our fuel consumption at 46mpg. It had been mostly motorway driving at between 65 and 70mph, so we were delighted. We reloaded the bags, and decided to check the oil, water and brake fluid, but all was OK. I noticed the chromed exhaust pipe had gone a nice blue/green colour. I like that, I thought.

We arrived on the Périphérique at about 5.30p.m. when people were leaving work. My goodness, if we thought the M25 was bad, this was far worse. It felt like the start of a stock car race – everyone seemed to drive so aggressively. I commented that this was a good way to learn Continental driving, but James didn't hear me as there was a lorry next to us blasting exhaust noise and fumes three feet from his face. It was then I remembered we had forgotten to pack the oxygen masks.

After an hour we turned off to the city centre, and in the distance we saw the Eiffel Tower. We had made it. James was having difficulty selecting third and fourth gears, which I thought was the clutch needing adjustment, but we decided to press on and look at it at our hotel.

We were on the Rue Renard going down towards the River Seine when James shouted that he couldn't get it in gear. I suggested trying second, but he had tried them all. We pushed

the car into the side of the road and soon had the bonnet off and tools spread out on the pavement. After 10 minutes work we decided it was not the clutch, and that it must be the gearbox. By this time we had a small crowd of interested onlookers, some of whom had brought their drinks over from the pavement café whose forecourt we were using. They all wanted to know about the problem. 'Kaput,' I explained. 'Wrong language; try "morte",' said James. This brought looks of sympathy whilst they sipped their wine. The crowd was growing, and then the patron of the café came out balancing a tray with two glasses and a bottle of wine for us, and would not accept any payment. By this time James had removed the remote control lever from the gearbox and found a bolt loose. Great, we could be on our way in 15 minutes.

Then two police motorcyclists arrived, and while the café patron poured their wine, the crowd explained to them what had happened. They asked for our destination, and when I showed them the brochure from our hotel, they knew it. While all this was going on, James had got the gear stick back in and the cover on. We started the engine, and as soon as it crackled into life a cheer went up. The patron fetched more bottles of wine and insisted we had one last drink. The policemen were determined to escort us to our hotel, and when we left the street party was in full swing. What a way to enter Paris in our new car, and with police outriders – we felt like royalty.

We had a wonderful couple of days visiting all the tourist spots, and wherever we went the car attracted attention – all of which we thoroughly enjoyed. The trip home was uneventful, and I even found room for some duty-free purchases. The car had been well and truly christened, and I was even reluctant to wash the wineglass rings off the bonnet.

The next car we are going to make will be a Bugatti replica. The French will really love that.

CHAPTER 17

Getting through the SVA

– a builder's story by Chris Rose

I am a 44-year-old pharmacist and a manager of a branch of Boots. In 1996 the original edition of this book inspired me to build and drive something a little more sporty than the family car. Although I had no engineering experience I had always enjoyed fiddling about with cars during my younger years and having read that 17-year-olds were creating Lotus 7 lookalikes I felt that I must have a go.

My wife Frances and my three daughters, Joanna, Elizabeth and Suzanne, all thought I had gone mad, but they gave me the green light and have been very supportive, with Frances being responsible for most of the car's upholstery. I am also grateful to my father, Les, and a neighbour, Jonathan Witney, a professional welder who lent me his MIG welder to get me started, some of his time and a lot of encouragement during the two-and-a-half years it took to turn a Mk II 1300cc Escort MoT failure into my very own sports car.

I thoroughly enjoyed the experience of building my own car.

I have learnt many new skills, such as panel beating and paint spraying, and would urge anybody, whatever their background, to do the same. I can now look forward to many years of driving pleasure, assuming that my wife and daughters haven't beaten me to the car keys!

I started to build my Locost in December 1996 and SVA legislation began to be phased in from 1 January 1998 (the SVA test became mandatory on 1 July 1998). As my

Fig. 17.1. Chris Rose (left) with his father-in-law. (Photo. Chris Rose)

build started well before this date and its test was to be before 1 January 2000, my car was dubbed a 'transitional provision vehicle' and as such it enjoyed a number of exemptions. These included dashboard projections, 19mm diameter dashboard support bar, exposed front suspension and an air filter protruding above the bonnet line. All these and many others are affected by regulations that builders who started after 1 January 1998 will have to consider. [For details of the test and exemptions see the Single Vehicle Approval Inspection Manual.]

To prove that I had started the build prior to 1 January 1998, I prepared a file of all relevant invoices prior to this date and took it with me to the SVA test. As it turned out the inspector did not look at it and took my word for it, but I still feel it is a good idea for builders to prepare this for the test, just in case.

THE TEST

Although I live in Chelmsford, Essex, my nearest SVA station is in Gillingham, Kent – a mere 120 mile round trip! Nevertheless, I duly booked my Locost in and hired a trailer to take it for its test on the day arranged. It failed, but only on two points both of which were easily rectified, and two days later I was back at Gillingham retaking the test (having put the car through the MoT which the Inspector insisted upon). This time the car passed and was issued with the necessary Minister's Approval Certificate. I then sent to my local Vehicle Registration office the paperwork, which consisted of MoT, SVA, insurance and chassis number certificates and receipts for parts and materials, vehicle registration form and cheque for road tax. I subsequently received the new registration number enabling me to put my Locost on the road. (The log book followed on from the DVLC at Swansea a few weeks later.)

One reason for failure the first time was that the rear view from the scuttle-mounted mirrors (from the wings of the donor Escort) was partially obscured by the rear wings. This problem was solved by fixing new wing mirrors to the windscreen supports. The other failing was the upper seat belt anchorage points which I had raised by welding in pillars made out of 5mm flat. To comply I had to fit supporting pieces to the rear to give greater strength and prevent any possibility of them bending forward in an accident.

I found the inspector at the test station to be extremely helpful. Mine was the first Locost he had tested. Prior to the test I had spoken to him on the phone and had sent him a 'builder's report' for his comments, which he gladly gave. In my case I was able to prove that the build had been started before 1 January 1998, which helped on some points. I felt that it was important to provide the inspector with as much advance information as possible, and to build up a picture of how I had constructed the car, and this certainly proved of value in my experience.

I had been concerned about the position of the front indicators as I had slung them beneath the headlamps (as suggested in the book) and the inspector confirmed that they were set too far back. I sorted this with some brackets welded to the chassis.

The Sierra servo unit which I fitted greatly improved stopping power and enabled the car to pass its brake test without problem. And, surprisingly, the CO test result was deemed better than some new cars by the inspector – not bad for an 85,000 mile Mk II Escort engine which had sat in a corner of my garage for over two years.

MY PRE-TEST NOTES TO THE INSPECTOR

Taking things in the order in which they appear in the SVA Inspection Manual, this is the 'builder's report' I sent to the inspector at the test centre.

Anti-theft device

The steering is from the donor Mk II Escort and incorporates the original steering lock. For additional security an electronic and/or an ignition cut out will be added later.

Defrosting/demisting

The original wiring loom containing the wiring to the heated rear screen and its switch was used in this vehicle and connected to the heated windscreen purchased from Caterham Cars. It operates effectively in severe weather conditions without fan assistance.

Windscreen wipers and washers

The wiper throws are correct, they park out of the line of sight and the wipers have two speeds, one of which exceeds 45 cycles/min. The washer system has a capacity in excess of one litre and the liquid is squirted on to the screen by means of an electric pump (all parts from donor vehicle) which clears the windscreen with the wipers working. The system also withstands plugged jets for between three and five seconds.

Seats

The seats are modified from the bases of the front seats and the back of the rear seat from the donor Escort. The bases are bolted through cross-members and the floor-pan. The cross-members are welded to the chassis sides. The seat back is held in place with brackets at the bottom and bolted through the upper rear boxframe with two nuts and bolts at the top.

Seat belts and anchorages

The seat belts have the minimum three anchorage points. Further to our recent telephone conversation and since the enclosed photographs were taken, I have raised the upper anchorage point to comply with the legislation. I have used the original upper anchorage, which like the other anchorage points consists of a 5mm thick fillet welded to the chassis and drilled. Each fillet has an appropriate nut welded to the rear surface to make fitting easier. The original upper anchorage was welded beneath the rear seat upper tube support. I have now bolted (using the old fillet and nut) and welded an additional 5mm pillar, drilled and an appropriate nut welded to the rear surface. The pillar each side now supports a bar across the back of the seats to which two headrests have been fitted. The seat belts themselves are from the donor car and so have the relevant markings to comply with the regulations.

The upper anchorage point now complies with the minimum 450mm above the reference point. The belts also have the facility to stow unwanted webbing.

Interior fittings
The handbrake is from the donor vehicle. All switches and knobs have been checked to comply with the regulations.

Radio suppression
All leads used are from the donor car and comply with the regulations.

Glazing
The windscreen was purchased from Caterham Cars and complies with the regulations.

Lighting/signalling
The correct operation and colour of lamps, their positions, etc., all comply with the regulations. The rear light clusters were purchased from Caterham Cars and incorporate a reflector. One fog lamp and two reversing lamps are fitted, purchased new. The headlamps are from a Citroën Diane and incorporate sidelights. The indicators have been fabricated using Mini indicators and have been repositioned further

forward, following our recent phone conversation and since the enclosed photographs were taken. The side repeaters are from a Volvo 340. The rear number plate light and boot light are from the donor vehicle (the entire loom from the donor was used) as are the dashboard lights, etc. The indicator relay unit from the donor was used and the hazard warning lights work with the ignition on or off.

Mirrors
The original wing mirrors from the donor car have been used (and turn inwards to comply) as has the interior rear-view mirror.

Tyres
The wheels and tyres are those used on the donor car and should therefore comply with these requirements.

Doors, latches, hinges
The only parts of the vehicle covered by this are the nose cone secured by Dzus fasteners (the two upper ones being covered by the bonnet), the bonnet itself (secured by 4 bonnet catches) and the boot secured by a barrel lock and key.

Exterior projections
The side-mounted exhaust provides the contact, which determines the floor line, and the jacking points do not project beyond the floor line by more than 10mm. The grille, wiper blades, wheels nuts and hubs all comply and the filler cap has been recessed.

Protective steering
The steering wheel is very smooth with no holes and has a deforming centre. The wheel is fitted with an energy-absorbing boss which would collapse on impact. The steering used is the original Mk II Escort column and shaft and has

been extended using an Allegro shaft with universal joints at either end which are offset from the column. The extended Allegro shaft has a puddle weld at either end of the steel tube for added strength.

Vehicle design and construction – general
The car's chassis, suspension and steering complies with the regulations, as does the fuel system. As for the electrical system, the original donor vehicle-wiring loom was used, and all joints, etc. have been insulated and the wiring connected together with either insulating tape or plastic ties.

Brakes
All hydraulic components including pipes and all components comprising the pedal box were used from the donor vehicle. The pedals have rubber caps. A servo unit and master cylinder from a Ford Sierra has been used to improve the braking as the donor car did not have servo assisted braking. The parking brake components are all from an Allegro and the system complies with the regulations. The original fluid level warning switch has also been used.

Noise
The car complies with the regulations.

Emissions (Petrol)
The car complies with the regulations.

Speedometer
The original instrument cluster and speedo cable have been used and should therefore comply with the regulations.

Design weights
The car complies with the regulations.

CHAPTER 18

Locost handling

by Rory Perrett

What I mean by the term handling is not ultimate road holding and the ability to go round corners as fast as possible. Handling is about the balance of the car, how it feels to drive. Good handling is a result of compromise, personal preference and what you want from your car.

If you want road holding, fit a set of wide wheels and tyres, clamp everything down and eliminate as much suspension movement as possible. Fit high rate springs and dampers and replace all those rubber bushes with something a lot harder. Great if you are one of our Locost Racing Series friends who just wants a race car. Not so good if you want to prevent your body and, more important, that of your passenger, being pulverised to a mush on that summer's evening drive to the local hostelry.

Racers want to minimise movement and reduce the variable effects of changes in the suspension geometry as the car is pushed to its limit around a circuit. Always try to keep in mind what you want the car for, change one thing at a time and maximise the benefit from the change before moving on to the next thing.

In the best Locost tradition, spending money is no guarantee of success, you could even end up with a car that is less to your liking than when you started. I'm sure that they won't thank me for

mentioning it, but if Mercedes can spend millions on their A Class and still get it wrong, then there's hope for us all.

There is a considerable amount of nonsense talked about the handling and set-up of cars. For most of us achieving the 'perfect' settings for camber, spring rates, etc. will not be an issue. Mild bump steer will not be noticed on our country drives, nor will that understeer which appears when trying to execute a right turn of a roundabout at 85mph. However, sensible changes can be made to improve your car and make it just that little more enjoyable for you to drive.

Static handling

It might seem a strange idea that one should have problems with the handling of a stationary vehicle, but good handling starts with weight distribution. The total weight carried by the tyres will always equal the total weight of the car and contents. While changing the total weight of the car is not an option, and here Locost builders have an advantage, you can affect the distribution of weight. However, and here is the first compromise, are you setting up with a full tank of fuel and two passengers or just the driver and half a tank?

Gauges for measuring the corner weights are available, although you might be able to get away with two bathroom scales and a suitable

cross member. A Locost, driver and half a tank of fuel will typically weigh 500kg to 600kg in total so you are going to need a range up to about 250kg to weight each corner. Remember that if you are weighing each corner in turn you need to chock under the other wheels to keep the car level. Ideally you want to achieve 25 per cent of the total weight on each wheel. Failing that, the corner weights should be equalised across each axle.

To achieve the weight distribution some items can be positioned favourably during the build. Consider fitting fuel tanks and batteries on the passenger side to help balance the weight of the driver along with wiper motors, heater boxes, etc.

For those who have splashed out on a set of shock absorbers with adjustable spring platforms, corner weights can be set by raising or lowering each spring seat. While remembering that keeping the ride height of the car as low as practical is an advantage, raise the spring platform to increase the weight on that wheel, lower it to reduce the weight. Don't be tempted to try to achieve an equal weight distribution across the wheels by having the shock absorber mounting brackets in different positions on each side.

Dynamic handling

Once on the move the way a car behaves is as a result of a set of complex interactions between the various elements and components which connect the car to the 'road'. These will change depending on the way in which the car is being driven and the 'road' it is being driven on. How the car stops, goes and steers comes down to the performance of the four tyres at the point where they are in contact with the road. The effect of any changes that are made to the suspension system and components must be considered in the context of how they affect the way the tyres do their job.

The ability of a tyre to perform is related to the 'grip' it can generate. If what we are asking of a tyre is less than the grip available then there is no problem. Demand more grip of any or all four of the tyres than is available, then you have got a problem.

The grip available from a tyre is related to the area of the tyre in contact with the road and the weight being carried by that tyre at the time. Of course, the road surface plays a big part as well but we generally have little or no control over that. The dynamic handling of the car comes down to the way in which the weight carried by each tyre changes as the car is driven (remembering that the total weight must stay the same).

A characteristic of tyre performance is that the grip from a tyre increases as the load on it increases. However, this effect is not linear. Doubling the load does not double the grip – the increase in grip is less than doubled. Similarly, halving the load means that the tyre has more than half the grip. Spread the load more evenly around the four wheels or between wheels on the same axle and you will have more overall grip. Making changes to help even out the weight distribution, especially when cornering, will help improve handling.

The basic design of a car is the first factor which has a fundamental effect on the way weight is redistributed during cornering, etc. and this is related to

the car's centre of gravity. Here the Locost is a winner before you start. As you go around a corner, weight is transferred to the outside wheels, the amount transferred depends upon the height of the centre of gravity and the width of the track. Low wide cars transfer less weight than tall narrow ones – back to the Mercedes A Class here. The Locost being more like a Formula I car than an A Class has the advantage. This advantage can be increased by keeping the ride height as low as practical and by mounting the engine and gearbox, fuel tank and driver as low as possible in the chassis.

Once your car is finished the options for altering the way weight is transferred and thus the handling is limited to component changes and adjustments within the suspension. Ron's Locost design does not include anti-roll bars, these being different to roll bars (cages) to save your head if you turn over your pride and joy – so the briefest of words. Anti-roll bars, front or rear, effectively connect the two wheels on one axle together. As one wheel raises or falls relative to the body the ant-roll bar causes the other wheel to do the same, levelling out the body. They change the weight transfer between axles by effectively stiffening up the axle with the roll bar giving the same result as fitting stiffer springs.

Turning to the changes and adjustments which are available within the Locost design, changing the rates of the springs fitted to your car can also be used to alter the weight transfer when driving. Fitting a higher rate (stronger) spring to a wheel will increase the weight carried by that wheel, a lower rated spring will reduce the weight carried. Higher spring rates will result in a harsher ride which is why car manufacturers prefer softer springs with anti roll-bars.

While the attitude of the car is changing, e.g. as it enters and leaves a corner, shock absorbers can be used to the same effect as springs. Stiff dampers will reduce

the rate at which the car reaches its roll angle and equilibrium. Until equilibrium is reached the stiffer shock absorber will act like a higher spring rate. Adjustable shock absorbers allow you to alter the rate at which the roll angle and equilibrium are reached.

Suspension geometry

Fitting wider tyres will increase the area of tyre on the road but could make the steering unacceptably heavy. Before you go for wider tyres, and probably wheels as well, it would be better to ensure that you have the maximum contact area from the tyres you have got.

When the car is not moving you will maximise the contact area by having the wheels vertical. However, you want maximum grip, not when the car is standing in the garage but when cornering. On road cars the suspension is not solidly attached to the car. Rubber bushes are used to reduce the level of shocks, vibration and noise transmitted to the body, which inevitably leads to some movement of the components when subjected to a load.

When cornering, the forces/load on the outside wheel will have a tendency to 'lean' out at the top, this is called positive camber. Setting a negative camber (the wheel leaning in at the top) when the car is static will allow the wheel to move to the vertical (zero camber) when under dynamic load when cornering.

The movement of the suspension up and down will also affect the camber angle of the wheel. Here we see how complex the relationship between the various elements of the suspension can be. The spring ratings affect the ultimate angle of body roll, while the dampers govern the speed at which that angle is reached, and the result also depends on the centre of gravity and the weight transfer. The suspension geometry, the movement in the suspension and the static camber angle will affect the camber of the wheels during cornering, as will the size of

Whoops – now that's understeer.

the tyre, the speed of the car and the tightness of the corner. Change one of these and you can affect all the rest.

Toe in or toe out is another adjustment like camber. A static setting of toe in on the front is set on rear wheel drive cars. Under driving conditions, movement in the suspension normally results in the front wheels moving towards zero toe.

Oversteer and understeer
Oversteer and understeer are much used terms in the motoring press. A well-balanced car should be neutral and display neither. However, manufacturers seem to consider that understeer is more desirable in the safety stakes than oversteer if neutrality under all conditions cannot be maintained.

Oversteer is where the car turns more than the driver expects from the amount the steering wheel has been turned. In terms of the tyres, it means that the front tyres are gripping more than the back. Under these conditions the car will tend to spin round – at least you won't be able to see what it is you are crashing into.

Understeer is the opposite in that the car turns less than expected and feels like it wants to go straight on rather than round the corner. The front tyres have less grip than the back and will skid first – you go off the road forward and benefit from grandstand seats for the ensuing accident.

For good handling, a set-up which gives neutral handling under most conditions, with a tendency to slight understeer when pushed, is considered the ideal. The following table might help you sort out a handling package that meets your needs.

Having made a component change, an adjustment may be required to the front wheel camber or toe to maximise the benefit. In general, wider tyres on the front will increase the forces on the suspension, requiring an increase in negative camber and toe in. Fitting uprated/harder springs/dampers or bushes will reduce suspension movement and mean a decrease in negative camber, and toe in is possible.

Whatever you do, have fun experimenting to get the car just as you want it. But, please, no tyre smoking, brake squealing and massive oversteer power slides in Sainsbury's car park just to see if that +1 deg camber change has done the trick!

To Reduce Oversteer (Increase understeer)	To Reduce Understeer (Increase oversteer)
• Increase front spring rate	• Decrease front spring rates
• Decrease rear spring rate	• Increase rear spring rates
• Stiffen front damper	• Soften front damper
• Soften rear damper	• Stiffen rear damper
• Increase rear tyre width	• Decrease rear tyre width
• Decrease front tyre width	• Increase front tyre width

CHAPTER 19

A disabled person's view

by Wally Woolven

You may have self doubts about constructing your Locost. I know I did. However, it was the thought of the challenge that inspired me. How's this for a scenario:

- I am 55. Do I need a hot rod?

- I am paralysed from the chest down and confined to a wheelchair.

- I cannot weld.

- I don't have a garage or workshop.

- I have no balance; support is always by holding on to the wheelchair with one hand or by leaning on some item – table or bench, etc. – with my forearms.

Despite this I now have a Locost rolling chassis. She sits wearing only a nose cone and scuttle and she is beautiful. Also, I am suffering from a terrible feeling of impatience. I want this car.

I won't give a blow-by-blow account but will include a few tips which I hope will help other disabled people, or those suffering from the self-doubt syndrome.

First, welding. A friend, on retirement, took a welding course and he said on many occasions: 'Come over and I'll teach you.' There followed a morning spent blowing holes in steel sheet. Bangs, splatter and the noise of frying … then molten metal running together. Strike out 'I cannot weld' from the above. And if I can do it …

I needed help. Friend Harry, also a car enthusiast, was approached. He agreed to help me, but should he build a kit, he in turn would expect my help. This was readily agreed.

The manageress of the Redditch Halcyon Day Centre was approached. Margaret listened and asked how much space I would need. I was told to go and clear myself an area. I was asked if Colin could help me. Colin was a stroke survivor in his mid-forties. A very determined guy, a definite asset.

After a day's blitz I had my area, locked cupboard, two carpentry benches and vices.

The next day I bought a MIG welder and an angle grinder, paid a deposit on a gas bottle and bought the gas. I also paid a visit to Worcester Steels, and lengths of RHS soon arrived. An 8 x 4 sheet of shuttering board was cadged off the maintenance section of the college. This was cleaned, painted and marked with the chassis outline. The board was then placed on four up-ended milk crates and levelled. I now have a base I can lean on to weld, clamp, cut, file, etc.

So, with Harry on Sundays and Colin during the week, the Locost chassis grew – despite Colin's comment that 'It'll never get off the ground.'

After searching for about a month, to no avail, for an Escort with auto transmission, I ran an advertisement in the local paper. She cost £50 – a non-runner Mark II 1300.

Wheelchairs are not very helpful when stripping cars. You can never get close enough. So, after a visit to the local fire station and a chat to the Chief Fire Officer, the guys of white watch in their Ferrari-painted fire engine paid the Day Centre a visit.

Coffee all round and then: 'Just suppose there was an accident victim trapped in that car, well this is how we would release him/her.' Twenty minutes later the 'Ferrari' was repacked with its equipment and crew, with the watch leader leaning out of the window saying, 'If you are ready by next Thursday, we will slip back and cut the rear axle out and chop the rest of the body up.'

Funny just how easy the engine and transmission came out, with the aid of a bath hoist, after white watch had left.

I also have a brother-in-law who is an engineer and an ace welder. Steve came over to check my cooking.

The Locost grew and so did our pride. My circle of friends also grew, including Malcolm of Dave's Autos (designer and builder of the A&M Kit Car, also supplier and builder of Ginetta sports cars) and the lads of Good Turn Engineering.

I went to their factory unit with some dimensions. Phil looked at it, 'Is this for 250 quid?' 'Yeah.' 'The seven series?' 'Yes, that's right,' I said.

On and on, scrap dealers, fastenings and fixing stockists, hire shops, etc.

Drivers have walked into the premises where our chassis now sits on its wheels awaiting some panel work. All want to know about it.

It has been a delight to build – the camaraderie and humour just terrific. I want the day to come when I drive it down to the fire station and show it off to white watch.

One last tip. Along with all the important protective clothing, goggles, etc., I recommend a baseball cap. Worn in the go-faster mode, i.e. back to front. This will stop hot sparks and grinding bits from going down your neck, and it will keep your hair in place when you try for your nought-to-sixty time on the car's completion.

You must be seriously thinking of building the Locost otherwise you wouldn't be reading this. All I can hope is that you get the same level of enjoyment and feeling of achievement that I have.

You can do it ... you know you can ... DO IT!

PART 6

GOING
RACING

CHAPTER 20

Racing a Locost

The Locost, with its very favourable power-to-weight ratio, makes the ideal basis for an entry-level club race car – a fact which has not escaped the eye of the RAC racing committee. There is now a Formula Locost race series run by the 750 Motor Club, and sponsored by Haynes, to encourage newcomers to construct and race their own cars. Its debut year was 1999 with six race meetings – two at Mallory Park and one each at Cadwell Park, Lydden Hill, Snetterton and Silverstone.

The Locost Series is for cars built as described in this book, subject to various safety modifications. The cars must be fully road legal and have a current MoT certificate, but you can remove the interior trim and passenger seat and it is permitted to use the passenger space for fixing a fire extinguisher, battery or roll bar bracing. Engines must be of Ford 'Kent' 1300cc type with block and head castings as produced, to which the only permitted modifications are a rebore of up to +0.090in, using standard-pattern pistons only, and replacement of valves, guides, seats and springs with parts of standard pattern and material.

If you are interested in racing, the first step is to contact the 750 Motor Club and ask for a Locost race series information sheet and a membership application form. The 750 Motor Club's Competitions Secretary is Robin Knight, West View, New Street, Stradbroke, Suffolk IP21 5JG (Tel: 01379 384268, Fax: 01379 384055).

If you are still keen after reading the information sheet, the next step is to join the 750 Motor Club. It is a prerequisite for any driver entering a motor race to be a member of an RACMSA (Royal Automobile Club Motor Sports Association) affiliated motor club, and the 750 Motor Club has been affiliated for the past 60 years. If you did not receive an application form with the fact

Fig. 20.1. An MSA 'Racing' starter pack. (Photo. Steve Williams)

sheet, write to Neil Carr-Jones, Membership Secretary, 750 Motor Club Ltd, Worth Farm, Little Horsted, Uckfield, East Sussex TH22 5TT. At the time of writing the cost of 12 months membership was £27.50 but there are concessions for under 17s, OAPs and for a partner. At the same time ask for a copy of the Locost Sporting Regulations.

Obtaining a competition licence

Before you can go racing you will need a competition licence. These are issued by the MSA (Motor Sports Association), the controlling body for motor sport in the UK. Write to them at Motor Sports House, Riverside Park, Colnbrook, Slough, Bucks SL3 OHG and ask for a starter pack for circuit racing. At the time of writing the pack costs £37 but it would be wise to check this first by telephone (01753 681736).

You will need to complete an ARDS (Association of Racing Driving Schools) course. These courses are run at most of the major British racing circuits. For example: Anglesey Racing Circuit, North Wales 01407 840253; Brands Hatch, Kent 01474 872331; Cadwell Park, Lincolnshire 01507 343248; Castle Combe, Wiltshire 01249 782417; Croft Circuit, North Yorkshire 01325 721815; Goodwood, West Sussex 01243 755060; Mallory Park, Leicestershire 01455 842931; Oulton Park, Cheshire 01829 760301; Pembrey Circuit, Carmarthenshire 01554 891042; Silverstone, Northamptonshire 01327 857271; Snetterton Circuit, Norfolk 0195 388 7303; Thruxton, Hampshire 01264 772696. The average cost for the course is £135.

You will also need to have a medical from your GP. When you have fufilled these requirements, send the forms back to the MSA, who will issue you with your licence. A National B licence, the type that you will need, costs £38.

With this you can compete on the racing circuits as a 'novice' driver. All 'novices' must display a black cross on a yellow square on the rear of their cars to indicate to other drivers that you are a new driver and gaining experience. After collecting ten 'race' signatures over a 24-month period you may remove the 'novice' sticker from your car.

Competitors' Yearbook

With the issue of your licence you will receive a copy of the *MSA Competitors' Yearbook* which is a fairly substantial volume containing in detail everything anyone needs to know about race rules and regulations and lots more besides. It is the race driver's bible. Race regulations are subject to revision each year and it is essential to work from the current edition of the yearbook.

Protective clothing

To comply with MSA safety criteria, clean flame-resistant overalls must be worn when racing. They should be made out of Nomex III, Proban or equivalent material and the label must show British Standard marks as listed in the Competitors' Yearbook.

You are also strongly advised to wear fire-resistant gloves, socks, balaclava and underwear. Do not wear man-made fibres as they are prone to melt in severe heat (cotton or wool is safer). It is advisable to wear proper race drivers' boots as plastic-soled shoes or trainers are prone to melt in high temperatures.

Your crash helmet should be in good serviceable condition and fit properly. The *MSA Competitors' Yearbook* lists acceptable helmet standards and MSA approval procedure. Be sure to check as standards are regularly reviewed and updated. Once approved a special sticker is applied to the right-hand side of the helmet by selected MSA scrutineers for which

Fig. 20.2. Examples of the regulation flame-resistant overalls which must be worn when racing. The picture was taken at Lyddon and shows (left to right) Darren Banks, Simon Pullan and James Champion who were respectively third, first and second in the Locost Series race that day. (Photo. Janet Pullan)

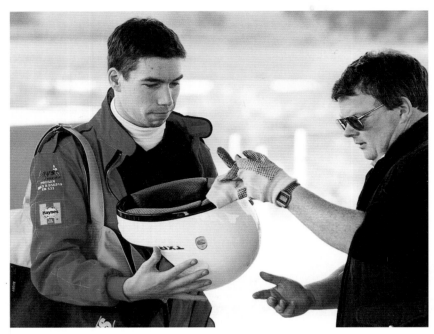

Fig. 20.3. A scrutineer checks James Champion's helmet prior to the race. Note the necessary MSA approval sticker. (Photo. Janet Pullan)

Fig. 20.4. Pre-race scrutineering at Lyddon Hill. A well prepared, well maintained and well presented car will put you on the right side of the scrutineer. (Photo. Janet Pullan)

a £1 fee is charged if your helmet was not bought ready-approved.

All race wear can be supplied by Jays Racewear and Embroidery, Department MSY, 363 Dogsthorpe Road, Peterborough, PE1 3RE (01733 568247).

Registration fee

Having joined the 750 Motor Club and when you are quite sure that your car will be ready for its first race or races, you need to register your car for the Locost Series. This will cost you £17.50. Contact the Competitions Secretary (see page 190).

Entry fees

Race entry fees may differ depending on the circuit but it is advisable to budget for a cost of £90 or £100 per race.

OBLIGATORY SAFETY MODIFICATIONS

Whether you have already built your car as a road-going sports car or you are planning to build one for racing only, you will of course need to make some modifications to the original design to comply with RACMSA safety regulations. What is required is listed in detail in the *MSA Competitors' Yearbook* and the Locost Sporting Regulations.

Roll cage

For racing you must fit a much more substantial roll bar than that for road use. The shape illustrated in the Yearbook is recommended as a minimum and it is stipulated that it must be made from cold drawn seamless carbon steel tube of 4.5mm diameter and 2.5mm wall thickness or 50mm diameter x 2mm wall thickness.

For Locost race cars I recommend making up a roll cage which is much stronger than the minimum requirement (see illustration). Refer to *Yellow Pages* for a local steel stockholder to source the specified tubing to make your own cage, or contact one of the specialist roll cage manufacturers such as Safety Devices Ltd, Regal Drive, Soham,

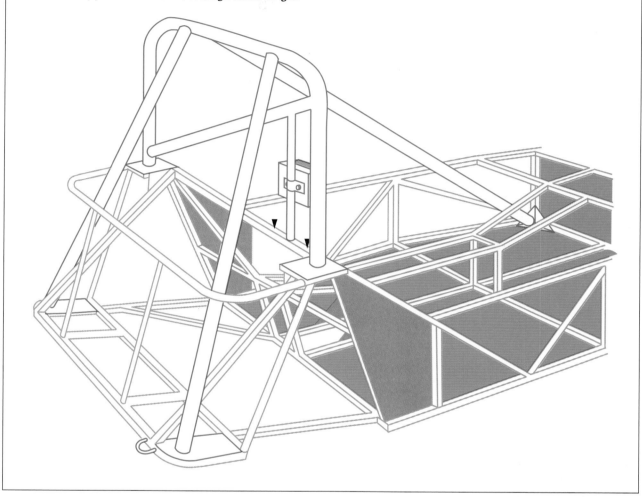

Fig. 20.5. Shows a roll cage in position, including an adjustable head restraint. Note the reinforcing plates at the roll bar mounting points. The drawing also shows a rear towing eye, and the black pointers indicate where the upper seat belt mountings need to go.

Cambridge CB7 5BE (01353 724202), Rollcentre, Somersham Road, St Ives, Cambs PE17 4LY (01480 464052) and Custom Cages of Daventry, Northants (01327 872855).

The tubing must be bent cold and the centreline radius must be at least three times the tube diameter. If the tubing is ovalised during bending the ratio of minor diameter to major diameter must be 0.9 or greater.

It is compulsory to include a strengthening tube running

Fig. 20.6. A welded upper roll cage mounting. (Photo. Steve Williams)

Fig. 20.7. A welded lower roll cage mounting. (Photo. Steve Williams)

Fig. 20.8. Front view of chassis showing roll cage in situ. Note the front towing eye welded to the lower bar of the front chassis member.

diagonally across the main roll bar hoop. The backstays are also compulsory and must be attached near the 'roofline' just before the outer bends of the main roll bar. They must be straight and run rearwards at an angle of at least 30° from the vertical. The frontstay in our design is not obligatory, but it has been included for extra rigidity and safety. All mounting points should be reinforced with steel plates and should be either welded or bolted in place.

Safety belts and head restraint

You must buy your seat safety belts as a complete unit from a recognised manufacturer (e.g. Safety Devices Ltd, see page 191) and they must be installed strictly as instructed by the manufacturers and in accordance with MSA recommendations or FIA requirements (see the *MSA Competitors' Yearbook* for these). The rear anchorage points should be arranged so that the straps extend to the driver's shoulders in as near horizontal a plane as possible. Do not mount the anchorage points on the floor directly behind the driving seat. The side anchorages should be fixed to the chassis (not the floor) to the left and right of the driver's seat.

Bear in mind that once involved in a serious accident seat belts should be replaced with new ones. They should also be changed if they come into contact with oil, acid or heat.

A head restraint which complies with MSA regulations must also be fitted so that your helmeted head cannot become trapped under the roll bar. These are easy to make and can be bolted to a vertical bar

Fig. 20.9. Rear view of chassis showing roll cage in situ. Note the towing eye.

Fig. 20.10. Rear safety belt mountings. (Photo. Steve Williams)

welded to the roll bar diagonal. This allows for up and down adjustment to suit driver height. For padding, use high density foam.

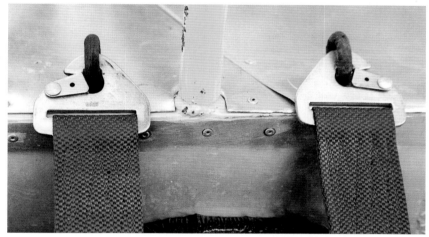

Fig. 20.11. Rear safety belt mountings with anchorage eyes and belts attached. (Photo. Steve Williams)

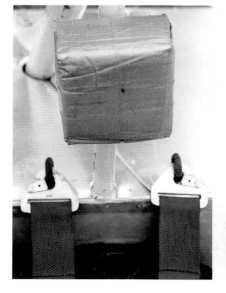

Fig. 20.12. Front and back of a head restraint bolted to a vertical bar between the chassis and roll bar hoop. (Photo. Steve Williams)

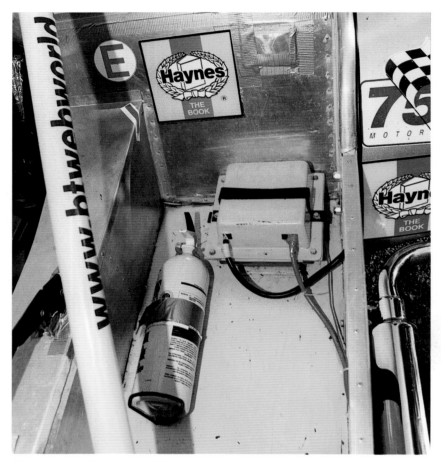

Fig. 20.13. A fire extinguisher mounted in the passenger compartment with a big red 'E' leaving no doubt as to its location. Also shown is a well-protected battery and a plastic holder for the scrutineer's 'Pass' card. (Photo. Steve Williams)

Fig. 20.14. A panelled-in fuel tank area, with access hatch. (Photo. Steve Williams)

Fire extinguisher

Your car must be equipped with a suitable in-car fire extinguisher which you can operate from your normal seated position, either manually or by a mechanical or electrical triggering system. It must be filled with an MSA approved extinguishant.

The extinguisher has to be retained in the car by positive quick release brackets secured by two bolts of at least 6mm diameter. Extinguishers with pressure gauges are recommended.

Red warning light

A rear red warning light compliant with MSA regulations (see *MSA Competitors' Yearbook*) must be located within 10cm of the centreline of your car and it must be clearly visible to following cars. When on the track the warning light must be switched on when conditions are such that visibility is reduced or when you are instructed to do so by the Clerk of the Course.

Fuel tank fillers, vents and caps

You must site your filler pipe and cap so that it does not protrude beyond the bodywork, and it must not be situated within the driver/passenger compartment. There must be an efficient locking action on the filler cap to ensure effective closing after refuelling and to reduce the risk of it flying open during an accident. Screw-on caps are best; any other type ought to have an additional locking device. Air vents must be at least 25cm to the rear of the cockpit and must be designed to prevent the escape of fuel should the car roll over. A non-return valve must be fitted and these can be obtained from the 750 Motor Club.

Since you will not be needing to refuel during races (which are only 12 laps at most), the filler pipe and cap does not need to be that accessible and for safety reasons it is obligatory that the fuel tank area is panelled in. A removable hatch can be fitted to access the filler, but this must be securely clipped down.

Fig. 20.15. Close up of removable hatch to fuel filler cap. Note the spring clips which secure the hatch. (Photo. Steve Williams)

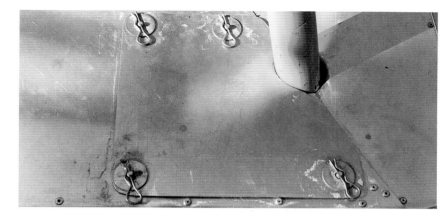

Fig. 20.16. Hatch removed to reveal filler cap. (Photo. Steve Williams)

Fig. 20.17. Shows a 750 Motor Club non-return valve. (Photo. Steve Williams)

Fig. 20.18. An external circuit breaker sited near the lower part of the windscreen mounting, duly labelled. (Photo. Steve Williams)

Fig. 20.19. Propshaft tunnel reinforcement to prevent injury to the driver in the event of a breakage.

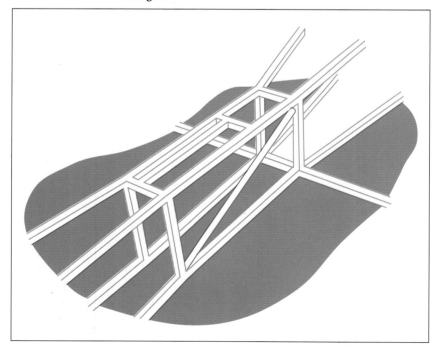

External circuit breaker

In case of an accident it is vital that the battery and all electrical circuits, with the exception of the fire extinguisher if this is electrically operated, can be immediately isolated from outside the car. The triggering system for the circuit breaker should be sited on the lower main loop of the rollover bar on the driver's side or at the lower part of the windscreen mounting. Its location must be identified by a red lightning flash on a blue triangle with a 12cm base (suitable transfers are obtainable), and the 'ON' and 'OFF' positions have to be clearly marked.

Propshaft restraint

To prevent injury in the event of a prop shaft failure a rigid steel reinforcement of at least 18swg thickness should be fixed around the transmission tunnel. The original chassis design is acceptable, but it is recommended that an additional diagonal is welded into place as an extra safety feature.

Exhaust pipe and exhaust noise

The exhaust system must comply with current MSA regulations and the outlet must terminate behind the midpoint of the wheelbase of the car and must be outside the bodywork periphery, but not protruding more than 4cm. Exhaust noise will be checked at race meetings and the limit is 105dB(A) with the engine running at ¾ maximum revs. The sound is measured at a distance of 0.5m from the exhaust pipe outlet and at an angle of 45° to its axis.

Some circuits have noise restrictions over and above this. Goodwood is an example. When testing there the cars were not allowed on to the circuit until they had passed a noise test, and to do this a device called a super trap had to be fitted to the exhaust tail pipe. This was necessary despite using a proprietary silencer which was deemed suitable for the public highway.

Fig. 20.20. Simon Pullan in the paddock at Mallory Park. Note the front towing hook and that the headlamps are taped in accordance with race regulations.

Towing eyes

To make it easy for the vehicle to be moved, substantial towing eyes must be fitted to the front and rear of the car no higher than 18in from ground level and they should be painted in a constrasting bright colour. Their position should also be indicated by the word 'TOW' on the body panelling.

Oil catch tank

Any breather pipes from the engine or rocker cover must be vented into a catch tank of at least two litres capacity.

Fig. 20.21. An example of an oil catch tank made from a suitably modified aluminium container. (Photo. Steve Williams)

Fig. 20.22. George Polley of George Polley Motors, agents for Yokohama tyres. He provides trackside service at most 750 Motor Club meetings.

Tyres

Remould tyres are not permitted for racing purposes, and re-cutting, re-grooving or any other way of modifying the tread pattern is prohibited. At the time of writing, the Locost Series regulations allow a choice of tyres from the MSA List 1A, but no alteration can be made to the manufacturer's specification. All the manufacturer's data must be clearly visible, and tyres must be to MoT requirements in every respect.

If the Series develops into a Championship it is very likely that a 'control' tyre will be stipulated and this is almost certain to be the Yokohama A509. Bearing this in mind it is suggested that you begin using these rather than buying any other. Contact the Yokohama agent for a competitor discounted price (George Polley Motors, Station Road Industrial Estate, Heathfield, E. Sussex TN21 8DB (Phone: 01435 863679/Fax: 01435 864354).

I have found that 22lb rear and 24lb front gives the best road holding, steering and braking response, although a lot of this is driver preference.

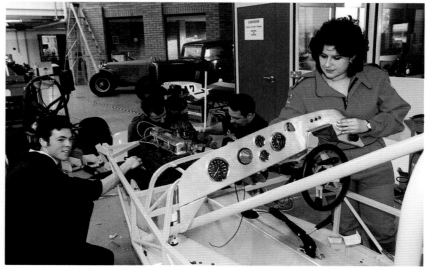

Fig. 20.23. The big amber light on this racing dashboard is an oil pressure warning light. In the heat of a race you may not see a small one.

Fig. 20.24. This engine mounting bracket is designed by Ian Gray of Stuart Taylor Motorsport. Although light in weight it is very strong. (Photo. Steve Williams)

HINTS AND TIPS

Oil surge can be a problem on the race-track, and you may find that you get the low oil pressure warning light showing on long sweeping bends at maximum speed. Centrifugal force throws the oil to one side of the sump leaving the oil pick-up pipe high and dry and sucking air. The position of your pick-up pipe to a large extent determines whether this happens most on left-hand or right-hand bends, but your weight in the driving seat is probably causing the car to lean a little more one way than the other. Whatever, the phenomenon is well known in the racing world. The problem can be solved by either using a baffled sump or something called a big wing sump which gives you extra oil capacity. Some have been known to tackle it by overfilling their engines with an extra pint of oil, but in my opinion this could do more harm than good. The only other alternative, a dry sump system, is out of bounds since it is prohibited in the Locost Series.

You will almost certainly experience fuel surge if you are using the one-baffle road car tank. The g-force generated in track racing calls for four or five baffles to overcome the problem. Even then you may still get trouble in extreme conditions and the solution could lie in changing the shape of the tank altogether. There is certainly no harm in using a much smaller tank. Most of the Locost races last only ten laps and as long as you remember to fill up after practising, a full two-gallon tank is going to give far fewer problems than a seven-gallon tank with two gallons sloshing about in the bottom.

Fig. 20.25. A back axle suspension bracket developed for racing. (Photo. Steve Williams)

171

Fig. 20.26. Nylon bushes which can be used in place of the metalastic road car bushes to improve road holding. (Photo. Steve Williams)

Suspension set-up

Set-up has a lot to do with individual preference, but a good starting point is to set the springs at 160lb rear and 300lb front, and to adjust all four shock absorbers to medium if conditions are dry and soft if it is wet. My practice is to set the spring bases so that there is equal travel both in compression and extension. Some very sophisticated (and expensive) electronic equipment is available which gives you a printout showing how much weight is on each tyre, enabling you to balance the car perfectly.

It is possible, I am told, to set the corner weights using four bathroom scales. Whichever method you use don't forget to make sure that you have on board your regular driver and race

Fig. 20.27. An alternative way to make bottom front suspension wishbones. Developed for racing by Martin Keenan of M.K. Mechanical Engineering, they are light and strong. (Photo. Steve Williams)

Fig. 20.28. An alternative way to make top front suspension wishbones. Also developed for racing by Martin Keenan of M.K. Mechanical Engineering. (Photo. Steve Williams)

Fig. 20.29. Also race bred by Martin Keenan of M.K. Mechanical Engineering are these square section rear suspension trailing arms. (Photo. Steve Williams)

quantities of water, petrol, oil and fire extinguisher, etc. The extent to which different sized drivers can affect the corner weights is surprising.

To tighten things up, replace the Triumph Spitfire/Herald suspension bushes (these can allow too much movement) used in the front wishbones, the rear trailing links and the Panhard rod with hard nylon bushes normally used for competition Spitfires and GT6s, etc.

Steering

I have found that setting the toe in at 1° works well, and a castor angle of 5° gives excellent self-centring whilst the steering still remains light with good feedback through the wheel.

Opinions vary on the camber angle. My starting point of 2° negative gives very good handling, although several people think that an extra degree might give better turn in.

The standard rubber bushes used in the steering rack brackets allow the rack to move slightly. If you want to eradicate this you will need to dispense with the Ford bushes and make up new brackets for a more positive fit. The reward will be sharper and more precise steering.

I leave fitting the steering rack until the whole car is built up and at its correct weight. Then I set the ride height and install the rack, ensuring that the track rod arms are horizontal. I drill two further sets of mounting holes in the rack mountings ¾in above and below the original mountings to give some adjustability. This seems to eradicate any bump steer.

Brakes

I fitted a dual circuit braking system with twin master cylinders and balance bar assembly using a modified standard Escort pedal box (see *Fig. 20.31*).

Fig. 20.30. For extra safety the steering rack mounting has been strengthened by the addition of a triangular side plate drilled for lightness.

Fig. 20.31. Twin master cylinders fitted to a much modified Escort pedal box incorporating a brake bias adjuster. Note the collapsible steering column.

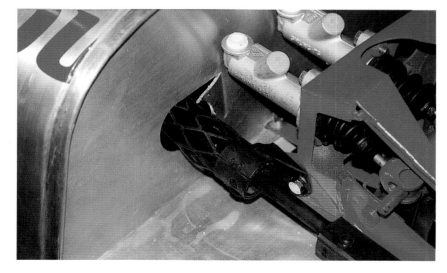

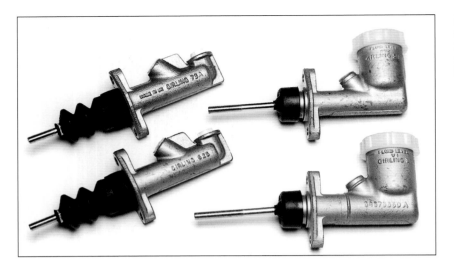

Fig. 20.32. Two types of master cylinder. The ones on the left are lighter and more compact but will need a remote plastic reservoir. (Photo. Steve Williams)

Exhaust system

An engine breathes through its exhaust pipe, and choosing or designing the right exhaust system will pay dividends in enhanced performance. To a large extent this is a matter of experimentation. Our four-two-one manifold proved effective.

I found that the cotton reel exhaust mounting, whilst fine for road cars, did not last very long on a race car. Hence a more substantial exhaust mounting is required. I now use a heavy woven fabric type of strap attached to a bracket, and this seems to work.

Fig. 20.33. Examples of strong exhaust mounting straps. (Photo. Steve Williams)

Fig. 20.34. I found that this exhaust manifold arrangement gave better top-end power. As can be seen, the bellhousing round the clutch and gearbox had been drilled to save weight, but the race scrutineers only let us get away with it once.

Seating

For additional safety and for comfort you can have a seat made up to exactly fit your body shape.

Windscreen

For racing it is not a good idea to leave the normal road car screen on the car as it is effectively an air brake and would put you at a distinct competitive disadvantage. You will need instead an aeroscreen designed and positioned so that the airflow, bugs, etc. are deflected over your head when racing. Such an item can easily be made up from perspex and secured to the car by alloy brackets.

Fig. 20.35. An example of a specially made cockpit seat moulded to fit the driver's body shape. The notches at the top are where the upper straps of the safety harness go. (Photo. Steve Williams)

Fig. 20.36. First-ever Locost race drivers' briefing. (Photo. Janet Pullan)

Fig. 20.37. That's cheating! Adam Wilkinson takes to the rough in an attempt (in vain as it happens) to pass James Champion. (Photo. Janet Pullan)

Fig. 20.38. Adam Wilkinson at Cadwell Park. Note the aeroscreen, the exhaust retaining strap, the Citroën 2CV headlights, the head restraint (attached to the roll cage diagonal on this car), the 4-2-1 exhaust manifold and the taped down bonnet catches. Note also that this car is not fitted with the 'belt and braces' front roll cage stay. (Photo. Janet Pullan)

Fig. 20.39. In the paddock at Mallory Park. Gordon Robbins (in blue overalls) talks to a fellow competitor. (Photo. Richard Whittaker Photography)

Fig. 20.40. Good tight racing as it should be. The last race of the 1999 season at Mallory Park. (Photo. Richard Whittaker Photography)

Fig. 20.41. Gentlemen, start your engines. (Photo. Mick Stone)

Warm-up lap, Lydden Hill. (Photo. Steve Williams)

SPONSORSHIP

Motor racing is an expensive sport even in the relatively less expensive Locost Series, but it is exciting to be involved with at any level and it attracts a lot of spectator interest. It certainly should appeal to your local newspaper, and most of them will include an article and photographs of a local person getting involved in the sport.

There is also good publicity potential for local businesses, especially your garage, tyre supplier, motor factors, race clothing suppliers and insurance brokers. Even solicitors nowadays are allowed to advertise their services. A Locost becomes a mobile advertising hoarding and the space can be sold. The best positions are the front and sides of the car and space here attracts the most money. One racer I know had his sponsor's name painted on the underside of his car where no one ever saw it until; on one sad occasion it rolled over in an accident and the sponsor was the provider of the roll cage which allowed him to walk safely away without a scratch.

Sponsorship need not always be by way of a cheque. Your sponsor may choose to provide you with a set of tyres, he may choose to paint your car or even supply your oil, disc pads and brake linings for the season, in return for his name on the car. You could probably arrange for him to have your car parked in his entrance hall, showroom or workshop for any special promotion that he might have, particularly if he is in the motor trade. The amount of sponsorship you can attract depends on having the right contacts and being able to capture a potential sponsor's enthusiasm and interest.

Motor Sport Association for the Disabled

The Motor Sport Association for the Disabled was formed in 1987 to assist the disabled, insulin dependent diabetics and those with other medical conditions to obtain competition licences from the MSA. If you are disabled or have a medical condition that you think might preclude you from holding a competition licence, contact David Butler, British Motor Sport Association for the Disabled, Bullscand Farm, Bullscand Lane, Chorleywood, Herts WD3 5BG.

PART 7

APPENDIX

Builders' cars

One thing's for sure, and that is that there are as many variations of Locost as there are builders who have made them. No two cars are alike, and what follows is a small selection of pictures of builders' cars which serves to bear this out and at the same time may give you some ideas and inspire you to become a Locost builder yourself.

The builder of this car successfully resolved the SVA inspector's concern over exposed lock-nuts on the track rods by nipping along to a nearby DIY shop and buying a short length of pipe lagging and four cable ties.

Meet the baby! Not content with the buzz he got from making a lifesize Locost, this builder went on to make a quarter-scale replica with working motor, and fully operational components.

Van den Plas, eat your heart out! How's this for luxury panelling? Note also the warm air vents which look well able to meet the windscreen demist/defrost requirements for the SVA.

Glassfibre is usually the material used to make the Locost nose cone, but this builder made his out of aluminium. He has also fitted side-screens and a hood (in the down position here).

Following publication of the original book, this was one of the first Locosts to be finished. The builder was aged 62 at the time and had never done anything on a car before.

Another example of side-screens. See also the plastic louvres set into the bonnet – saves the laborious procedure of cutting your own.

Here's one with a hood in place. The builder of this car is a big guy and he made it six inches wider and six inches longer than the standard size Locost.

Although you can't see it, there's a perspex panel framed by the roll bar, and he plans to fit gull-wing doors using the horizontal overhead bars as pivots.

Although this is a road car, it looks like a racer with its aero screens and driver's name painted on the side.

Is it a windscreen or is it an aero screen? An interesting variation, as is the hinged bonnet.

Built to a budget, and very much in the image of the original car as shown on the cover of the first edition of this book. Note that the donor Escort wheels have been used.

Interesting features on this car include the spare wheel carrier, the security box built into the boot, the dashboard, aero screens and flared front wings.

Another example of flared front wings, but the interesting feature on this particular Locost is the offside perspex wind deflector.

This rather special Locost was built by one of my pupils. The two younger boys looking on are probably thinking 'I'm going to make one like that.' By now they probably have.

Another pupil showing off the fruits of his automotive creativity to his father (background) at a school open day.

Any colour you like, as long as it's black ... and yellow! Combined with the bright yellow wings and nose cone it makes this Locost look particularly distinguished, and the chequerboard decal is a masterstroke.

A sleek-looking car made sleeker by its flush-fitting air filter. This one, too, has perspex wind deflectors.

Simple clean lines are the distinguishing feature of this builder's car.

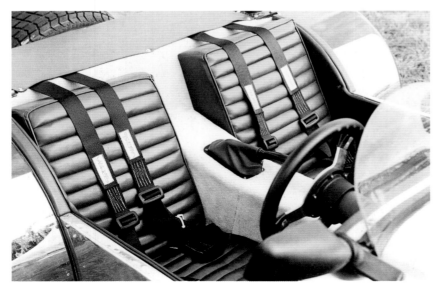

Here's what it looks like inside. A nice clean job.

The mother of all Locosts! Would you believe 300bhp sits under this specially made bonnet?

Seeing is believing! The 300bhp engine revealed.

You don't have to have fancy wheels to achieve stunning looks. The smartness of this car is more than a match for the picturesque backdrop.

There's more than one use for an exterior mirror! Now, where's that SVA inspector?

The author showing off a Locost racer to Lt.Com. Jez Spring at the Navy Training Establishment at HMS Gosport, and trying to do a deal for home-to-circuit transport! (Photo. Neil Carr-Jones)

A smart racer, first time out at Mallory Park in October 1999. (Photo. Richard Whittaker Photography)

Variations on a theme.
(Photos. Steve Williams)

Useful addresses

CLUBS

Locost Car Club
PO Box 428
Stilton
Peterborough PE7 3ZA

The Locost Car Club is run by builders and owners of Locosts for builders and owners and exists to provide help, information and support at any stage of your Locost build. Send a large SAE for full details, membership list, newsletter, help and advice and details of runs, rallies and races.

750 Motor Club
Membership Secretary
Neil Carr-Jones
Worth Farm
Little Horsted
Uckfield
East Sussex TH22 5TT
Tel. 01825 750760

Competitions Secretary
Robin Knight
West View
New Street
Stradbroke
Suffolk IP21 5JG
Tel. 01379 384268

The Locost Race Series, sponsored by Haynes and run by the 750 Motor Club, features cars built by amateur constructors to plans featured in this book.

British Motor Sport Association for the Disabled
David Butler
Bullscand Farm
Bullscand Lane
Chorleywood
Herts WD3 5BG
Tel. 01923 285554

Norsk Locost Car Club
Askimvn.218
1408 Kråkstad
Norway
Tel. 917 85 971

SUPPLIERS

M.K. Mechanical Engineering
2 Addison Road
Maltby
Rotherham S66 8DG
Tel. 01709 815740

MIG and TIG welding specialists in steel and aluminium. Supplier of Locost chassis, suspension units, fuel tanks, nose cones, mudguards, etc.

Racers Hardware
8 South Street
Crowland
Peterborough
Lincs PE6 0AJ
Tel. 01733 211311

Suppliers of shock absorbers, Aurora rod ends, and aluminium seats.

Ron Champion
'The home of the Locost'
Speed Consultants Ltd
Showroom 1
Midland Road
Peterborough PE3 6DD
Tel. 07887 723482
www.ronchampion.com
ron@ronchampion.com

Stuart Taylor Motorsport
9 Slade Close
Ilkeston
Derbyshire DE7 4PB
Tel. 0115 9399497

Suppliers of chassis, suspension units, glassfibre and all other parts for road and race Locosts.

Demon Tweeks
75 Ash Road South
Wrexham Industrial Estate
Wrexham
North Wales LL13 9UG
Tel. 0800 854794

Mail order supplier of all motor sport needs.

George Polley Motors
Station Road Industrial Estate
Heathfield
East Sussex TN21 8DB
Tel. 01435 863679

Road and race wheel and tyre centre. Trackside service at most 750 Motor Club meetings. Agent for Yokohama tyres.

Jays Racewear and Embroidery
Department MSY
363 Dogsthorpe Road
Peterborough PE1 3RE
Tel. 01733 568247

Suppliers of race wear.

Safety Devices Ltd
Regal Drive
Soham
Cambridge CB7 5BE
Tel. 01353 724202

Specialist roll cage manufacturers.

PHOTOGRAPHERS

Photographers who regularly attend Locost Series race meetings.

Steve Williams
Tel. 01733 840471/0585 206022

Richard Whittaker
Tel. 0113 3688056

Janet Pullan
Tel. 01785 712751

SPECIALIST INSURANCE COMPANIES

Kit car specialists:

Footman James
Waterfall Lane
Cradley Heath
West Midlands B64 6PU
Tel. 0121 561 4196

Provides quality cover at competitive premiums with inclusive UK and Continental breakdown recovery plus road rage personal accident cover and legal expenses.

Snowball Insurance Services
Tel. 01922 686116

Competition car specialists:

Competition Car Insurance
Tel. 0115 941 5255

The addresses and telephone numbers were believed to be correct at the time of going to press. However, as these are subject to change, particularly telephone area codes, no guarantee can be given for their continued accuracy.

Recommended reading

750 Racer: Everything you need to know about building and racing a low-cost sports-racing car, Peter Herbert with Dick Harvey (Haynes)
Advanced Race Car Suspension Development, Steve Smith (Autosports Publications)
Automotive Brake Manual (Haynes)
Automotive Electrical and Electronic Systems Manual (Haynes)
Automotive Glassfibre, Dennis Foy (Bluestream Books)

Automotive Welding Manual (Haynes)
Brake Handbook, Fred Puhn (HP Books)
Competition Car Preparation: a practical handbook, Simon McBeath (Haynes)
Competition Car Suspension, Allan Staniforth (Haynes)
Ford Escort and Cortina Purchase and Restoration Guide, Kim Henson (Haynes)
How to Make Your Car Handle (Bluestream Books)

Race and Rally Car Source Book, Allan Staniforth (Haynes)
Race Car Chassis, Forbes Aird (Motorbooks International)
Rebuilding and Tuning Ford's Kent Crossflow Engine, Peter and Valerie Wallage (Haynes)
Soldering, Brazing and Welding (Bluestream Books)
The Metal Fabricators Handbook, Ron and Sue Fournier (HP Books)
Weber Carburettors, Pat Braden (Bluestream Books)

Useful books from Haynes

Rebuilding and Tuning Ford's Kent Crossflow Engine
BY Peter & Valerie Wallage

Since first appearing in 1967, the immensely popular Kent Crossflow engine has been used to power various models of Cortina, Capri, Escort and, in transverse form, the XR2 Fiesta. It has been an option for kitcars, also achieving lasting fame in motorsport. This book covers the history of the Kent engine; rebuilding and tuning (both mild and serious) in the home garage; performance exhaust systems; uprating the ignition system; and overhauling and fitting a Weber DGAV 32/36 carburettor.
ISBN: 1 85010 938 9   **£17.99** RRP

Automotive Brake Manual
Maintenance and repair techniques for automotive braking systems. Step-by-step brake pad and shoe replacement procedures covering all popular cars and light commercial vehicles. Explains the principles of braking system operation plus the fundamentals of ABS and hydraulic systems.
ISBN: 1 85960 202 9   **£14.99** RRP

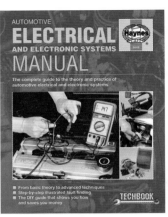

Automotive Electrical and Electronic Systems Manual
Guide to the essential theory and practice for all car electrical and electronic systems. Covers charging systems, starter motors, batteries, instruments, displays, lighting, signalling and ignition systems. Includes fault finding information and vehicle wiring diagrams.
ISBN: 1 85960 049 2   **£14.99** RRP

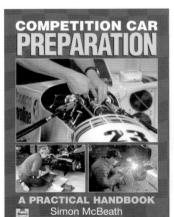

Competition Car Preparation: A practical handbook
BY Simon McBeath
FOREWORD BY Ray Mallock

Taking case studies from a wide range of competition car categories, this book covers everything from planning, budgeting, driver licencing and tuition, to all the practical aspects of getting a car and its driver into the best state of preparation affordable for successful competition, and keeping them that way. In series with *Competition Car Downforce* and *Competition Car Composites*.
ISBN: 1 85960 609 1   **£19.99** RRP

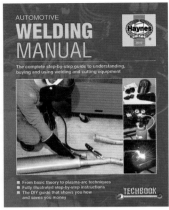

Automotive Welding Manual
Basic guide to gas, arc, MIG, TIG and plasma welding and cutting techniques. Covers basic theory and safety procedures, choosing and using welding equipment and a glossary of welding terms.
ISBN: 1 85960 201 0   **£14.99** RRP

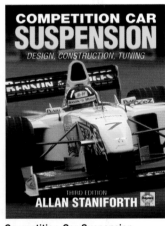

Competition Car Suspension
(3rd Edition): **Design, construction, tuning** BY Allan Staniforth

The author, a long-acknowledged expert on the subject, explains the theory and practice of successful suspension engineering, and explores in an easy-to-understand and readable style how and why suspension systems work. Since the first edition the banning of active suspension from motor racing has been a strong spur to damper design. This third edition has been fully updated to include the latest developments and is the result of considerable research.
ISBN: 1 85960 644 X   **£19.99** RRP

Race and Rally Car Source Book
(4th Edition): **The guide to building or modifying a competition car**
BY Allan Staniforth

A thorough guide to the DIY building and modifying of a car for racing or rallying. Describes champion circuit, rally and hillclimb cars from Formula 750 to Formula 1. **'If you are a serious competitor in either race, rally or hillclimbing this is an excellent addition to the tool box'** *Cars & Car Conversions*
'Simple and easy to follow, it is a must for any club competitor' *Auto Express*
ISBN: 0 85429 984 X   **£19.99** RRP

750 Racer: Everything you need to know about building and racing a low-cost sports-racing car
BY Peter Herbert in association with Dick Harvey

Packed with information and anecdotes, this is about how, for the price of a small second-hand road car, you can build a competitive 750 racing car, and run it for a season for the cost of a Continental family holiday.
ISBN: 1 85260 447 6   **£17.99** RRP

These books are available from most highstreet bookshops, branches of Halfords, or direct from the publisher.

Haynes Publishing, Sparkford, Nr Yeovil, Somerset BA22 7JJ
Telephone: **01963 442030** • Fax: **01963 440001** • E-mail: **sales@haynes-manuals.co.uk**
Web site: **www.haynes.co.uk**